# STICKS
# &
# STONES

# STICKS
# &
# STONES

## How Digital Reputations Are Created Over Time and Lost in a Click

LARRY WEBER

**WILEY**

John Wiley & Sons, Inc.

ISBN: 978-0-470-45738-2 (cloth)

Printed in the United States of America.

10 9 8 7 6 5 4 3 2 1

Dedicated to my parents, Vern and Beverly
*Vobis gratias pro vita discendi et amoris ago*

# CONTENTS

# FOREWORD

A generation ago, the radical activist Abbie Hoffman penned a manifesto called *Steal This Book!* He wanted to change the way the world worked, and his starting point was this manual for building a new society. That was then, of course, and this is now. Hoffman wasn't right about much, though the world he hoped to change is long gone. The driver of this change is not 60s-style radicalism but a host of factors, the most important of which is the backdrop of Larry Weber's new book. The digitization of everything, especially "the media," has rendered long-standing ways of organizing, working, communicating, and competing obsolete. I'm sure Larry doesn't want you to steal *Sticks & Stones*, but I can't urge you strongly enough to read it. It's a manual for prospering in a new society.

Companies today must navigate troubled waters, which are roiled not only by a deep recession at the moment, but also by longer-term currents. The Internet, the 24/7 news cycle, social computing and blogging, the omnipresence of watchdog groups, a proliferation of controversial, high-stakes issues on which companies are expected to have public positions—think climate change, energy efficiency, HIV/AIDS, global poverty, malnutrition, obesity, water availability, quality, and rights, to name just a few—all these combine to make the business environment a more dangerous, less forgiving, less tractable place. In this new world, critics are poised to attack and hostile constituencies can mobilize instantly, with devastating impact. Corporate reputations and valuations are at much greater risk than ever before. Welcome, as Larry says, to World 2.0.

World 2.0 is a manifestation of the latest, still rapidly evolving digital technology, which enables information (not necessarily accurate) to move everywhere at the speed of light. It's worth adding that this world also is highly competitive, which compounds the dangers. Long gone are protected markets, regulated monopolies, and administered economies that provided walls behind which complacent companies could be shielded. Today, competition nearly everywhere on the planet is fierce and relentless and companies are under high pressure constantly to upgrade their capabilities and improve their operations. Meanwhile, the basis of competitive success in World 2.0 has shifted. It used to be that competitive advantage was built on hard assets like natural resources, money, and plant and equipment. Now and in the future, the basis of advantage consists of the so-called soft assets: human assets and the intangibles, knowledge assets and social assets. Among the latter, a company's reputation is one of its greatest and most valuable. Even in today's down markets, a dominant share of the worth of great companies like Procter & Gamble, Toyota, Johnson & Johnson, and many others consists of goodwill and other intangibles.

In World 2.0 the reputations of companies and the individuals who work for them are subject to swift, sometimes irreversible, damage. Consider Yum Brands, corporate parent of several leading fast-food chains, as Larry recounts in Chapter 2. In 2007, a late-night passerby noticed a swarm of rats scrounging for food in a closed KFC/Taco Bell. This individual alerted a local New York TV station and in less than twelve hours the broadcast story went viral on YouTube. During the next two weeks, Yum Brands watched its stock plunge by nearly 10 percent. While the stock eventually recovered, the story still circulates on the Web, with over a million viewers to date.

At about the same time Yum Brands suffered its reversal, the energy giant BP faced a series of setbacks—fatalities in a refinery explosion, leaky oil pipes in the wilderness, tax disputes with foreign governments—that could have ruined a company with a lesser reputation. Yet BP under John Browne had spent more than a decade building and guarding a new reputation as a different kind of energy company, moving "beyond petroleum" and becoming an environmental champion. When the bad news hit, BP suffered but not for long, as its goodwill with environmentalists and communities enabled the setbacks to be viewed in a larger context as mistakes and accidents occurring at a fundamentally good company.

*Sticks and Stones* is a guide to surviving and thriving in World 2.0. The good news is that companies don't have to watch passively and suffer what comes. In fact, if they follow Larry's advice—that of a seasoned and highly successful entrepreneur and business leader—they can build stronger reputations, anticipate problems and crises, and monitor and manage the commentary "out there" in cyberspace. It starts with a company's moral purpose—its higher calling that transcends its specific objective to make money. When its moral purpose is authentic and stated clearly and pursued consistently, employees are more focused and determined to succeed. External constituencies are more willing to convey their respect and trust, or at least give the benefit of the doubt. This is a potent and evergreen source of competitive advantage.

Armed with an authentic moral purpose, companies can then build and protect their reputational equity—by forming and moderating digital communities, using blogs and other tools to form and shape their digital rep. The technology is proven and readily available, and companies run unnecessary risks if they don't tap what their potential critics know very well how to use. Worse, they don't take advantage of tools that can help them form and deepen relationships with customers, suppliers, and other constituencies. It doesn't take much time or investment to monitor Twitter or YouTube or to post a steady stream of fresh content on your own, friendly, or neutral sites. Yet the benefit can be substantial.

Larry endorses a colleague's belief that companies ought to consider themselves as permanently in pre-crisis mode. Do you have the tools and techniques in place, do you know where to go, to squash rumors before they morph into threats? To respond instantaneously to a real threat? To plant your views in cyberspace? To form sympathetic digital communities? To build a deep reservoir of goodwill? If so, you can prosper in World 2.0. If not, you'd better listen to Larry.

—Mark B. Fuller, chairman, Monitor Group

# PREFACE

For the past 30 years I have been a student of the media and marketing. I've advised hundreds of companies of all different sizes and industries, helping them navigate a wide spectrum of business challenges and marketing opportunities. Along the way, I built the world's largest public relations agency and made numerous acquisitions and investments in other PR firms and marketing services companies.

It's been a fascinating journey that has afforded me a crow's nest view of the evolution of reputation management, influence and brand. In the past decade the rapid rise of digital media (blogs, social networks, e-communities) has transformed the media landscape. More and more people get their news and entertainment online; print newspapers, magazines, and the nightly TV news are dying a slow death. Now, thanks to the Web, anyone, anywhere, and at any time can be a publisher, producer, or distributor of content. As a result of this uncontrolled explosion of information and opinion, reputations can be made or destroyed overnight with a few clicks of the mouse. It feels a lot like the Wild West and no one knows who the last man or woman standing will be.

I wrote this book because CEOs, CMOs, and other professional communicators keep asking me to help them understand and succeed in this chaotic landscape. In my travels, I'm frequently asked questions such as "Larry, should my company start a corporate blog?," "Larry, should we form a Facebook group?," "Larry, does Twitter really matter?"

Given the enormous media attention and valuations of companies like Google and Facebook, these questions are not surprising—and

I will address them in this book. However, I think that they are just the tip of the proverbial iceberg and that the real issues go a lot deeper. We are at a point in time where there needs to be a complete change in how businesses organize and how they interact with their key stakeholders.

In the traditional model, corporations exercised a large degree of control over their brands, and reputation was separate from brand. In the digital age, the pendulum has swung and it's now customers and other stakeholders who have the power to impact and shape a brand through conversations – both on and offline. I call this dialog branding. Influence and brand are now converging and together determine reputation.

To be successful in this new environment, businesses must engage transparently and authentically with their key constituencies. They require strategies for content creation, distribution, and engagement. Most important, businesses need to get deep in their bones that this is not just the responsibility of the marketing and corporate communications departments. While those two groups have traditionally served as the stewards of the brand, the new landscape impacts the entire organization and demands new approaches to how businesses organize.

The great thing about the Web is that after reading this book we can continue this conversation. I look forward to listening to your opinions and ideas so that together we can discover even more ways to leverage new media and build great brands.

—Larry Weber
Boston, Massachusetts

# Digital World, Digital Reputation

# Your Digital Reputation in World 2.0

The childhood taunt got it half right. Sticks and stones *will* break your bones, but words *can* hurt you. Just ask a former Arthur Anderson employee, a Mattel executive, or Chick Edwards. Who, you ask, is Chick Edwards?

Chick Edwards is the owner and developer of a 47-lot subdivision in Kennewick, Washington. In late 2007, he sold one of his houses to an Army reservist who moved in with his wife and young son. In mid-2008, the reservist was called to active duty and his then-pregnant wife and son moved to be with her family on the East Coast. They left behind a weed-filled 2.5-acre lot that had not been landscaped. Edwards was not happy.

He told a local newspaper reporter, "I really don't give a (expletive) where he is or what his problem is. It doesn't matter to me." Edwards insisted that the reservist had violated homeowner's association covenants that required landscaping be completed within a year after a home's occupancy permit is issued. The reservist "doesn't have the right to walk away from his obligation," said Edwards. As the developer, he is the only member of the homeowners' association. "I have most of the property still, so I am the homeowners' association," he told the reporter. The article concluded with a final Edwards' quote: "This is a contract. I don't like the way his property looks. This clown gets to do what he wants, and I'm mad as hell."

If the story had gone no further than the print edition of the *Tri-City Herald*, I'm sure it would have caused a stir—angry readers, a few letters to the editor perhaps—but we are in World 2.0, and that makes all the difference. The story went up on the paper's web site where people could comment, and they did.

"Sorry you're such an awful, awful person . . . maybe you'll learn when no one else buys your lots, you *******."

"I for one will let everyone I know NOT to even consider purchasing a lot from you. You can have your development all to yourself. You deserve yourself as a neighbor."

"I can't understand how you could be so cold! Mr. Edwards I think you should have to take Lt. Jensen's place in Kuwait while he comes home to clean up his yard for you."

"You are not worthy to be living in the United States that our sons and daughters are fighting for right now. May God, karma, or whatever you believe in come full circle and bite you where you live."

One of the people commenting posted Edwards' phone number and web site address—something no responsible newspaper editor would do—and called for others to tell Edwards directly how they felt about him. An updated newspaper article added this quote from a potential homebuyer: "I am simply amazed that a member of this community can think that treating people like this will gain them recognition or business in some way. My wife and I are in the market for a new home with a couple of acres of land, but I will be sure to skip this offering while looking."

Even worse, the story was no longer local: A Seattle radio station picked it up and interviewed Edwards on the air, where he excused his intemperate remarks by saying he'd been having "a bad hair day" when he spoke to the newspaper reporter. *The Seattle Times* picked up the story, and two days later, it was still the most-read article on that paper's site (and its readers also had some harsh things to say about Edwards).

The story also hit social sites like plime.com and craigslist, and attracted blog commentary from as far away as Chicago (and now it's in a book). According to Matt McGee, who writes about small business marketing, Edwards was getting bombarded with angry e-mails and eventually stopped answering his phone. "Although local real estate agents would never admit to it," says McGee, "chances are good that a lot of them would warn their clients about moving into Edwards' development. And he has about zero chance of ever restoring the Google search engine results position on a search for his name." So much for any reputation as a conscientious, hard-working member of the community.[1]

## Welcome to World 2.0

Globalization, sustainability, corporate responsibility, and financial transparency are major trends impacting the way that organizations engage their employees, customers, partners, investors, and other key constituencies. At the same time, the explosion of social networks, e-communities, and the blogosphere are dramatically transforming the communications landscape; both traditional and social media are dynamically forging new vehicles for the creation and distribution of content.

This is World 2.0, the evolving environment that businesses have to understand if they are to be productive and survive. We are evolving from the way things *were* done to a new way of doing things. We saw it in politics with the Obama presidential campaign. We are seeing it in healthcare; old pharma now having to understand DNA-based development. We are seeing it in technology; the Internet is moving into Web 2.0 with new tools. We are seeing the decline of newspaper and television news due to more user-generated and web-based instant distribution and access to news and information.

Senior executives are talking about moral purpose. What should the company stand for? What is our reputation? They realize the organization will be judged in part on their ethics and their morality.

The way companies organize around their customers is changing. They have to listen to their complaints, suggestions, and ideas in a way they did not have to, say, twenty years ago. They have to engage in dialogue with customers, so marketing is changing radically. Customers—indeed all stakeholders—demand transparency, authenticity, and responsiveness from the organizations they care about.

True, there was always some demand for transparency, authenticity, and responsiveness but, compared to today, it was weak, localized, and ineffective. Today you can't hide. You also can't just shout from the highest mountaintop about how great you are. Today organizations have to show modesty, understanding, and a willingness to listen. Understand that you are going to be doing business more transparently and accept that you have lost control, if you ever really had that much control anyway. Conversations are happening all around you, your market, and your company. All C-level executives will have to understand the new forces shaping the environment in which they work if they hope to survive.

As an extension of World 2.0, you should understand that the Web is not a channel—it's not like a television set or a billboard. I believe the digital universe is just as important as, or equal to, the physical world. So the Web and how you and the organization relate to it is not simply marketing's assignment or an information technology function. It affects individuals and the entire organization, whether a small business or a large corporation.

## The Risks to Reputation

What is more important than a positive personal, professional, and corporate reputation? A good reputation builds customer loyalty, helps attract talented employees, and earns shareholder confidence. As recent economic history has demonstrated, banks that don't trust each another—"trust" being a key element in one's reputation—won't loan money. In a very real sense, a good reputation is a lot like money in the bank.

"Reputation risk may well be the biggest risk challenge facing global companies today," Ansi Vallens said in a recent *Risk Management* article. In the 2005 study Vallens cited, 52 percent of the 269 risk executives surveyed said that reputation risk was more significant than regulatory risk (41 percent), human capital risk (41 percent), IT risk (35 percent), market risk (32 percent), and credit risk (29 percent). These executives spoke from experience: 28 percent reported that their firms had suffered major financial loss from a reputation-damaging event.[2]

Unfortunately, your reputation is not something you can control like product quality, service response time, advertising taglines, or the research and development budget. Although everything you do—or don't do—can affect your reputation, ultimately it's all about how customers, employees, suppliers, shareholders, and regulators perceive you or your company. Good, bad, or indifferent, your reputation resides in *their* minds.

According to an annual Harris Interactive survey released in June 2008, seven out of 11 industries saw their reputation decline in 2007 from 2006's ranking, and 16 of the companies with the worst marks fell even further. At the same time, the study found "a strong statistical correlation exists between a company's overall reputation and the likelihood that consumers will purchase, recommend or invest in a company or its products and services." Robert Fronk, senior vice president, senior consultant, reputation strategy at Harris Interactive, says that the survey "has shown in recent years that companies that pay attention to enhancing their reputation see bottom line results. The companies with a good reputation have stayed near the top of the list and those with bad reputations have gotten worse."

Ken Powell, chairman and CEO of General Mills, notes, "Reputation can be measured in recognition, employee recruitment and retention, even stock price multiple. But in the end, we believe the most important measure is trust. General Mills values its reputation tremendously, and we constantly strive to remain worthy of the trust of our customers, consumers, employees, investors and communities."[3]

Because reputation is not based on facts or hard data, Vallens notes, reputation risk can be difficult to identify: "Why is it that some companies are punished for not achieving expected earnings, while other companies make gains even if their earnings fall short? In many cases, the winning companies not only recognize the value of reputation, but actively manage it. The U.S. auto industry is a good example. Though quality levels for American-made cars now rival those manufactured in Japan, the Japanese cars still lead in reputation. Why? Because the Japanese automakers understand that reputation is their greatest asset."

## Reputation Equity

Honda, Toyota, and Renault-Nissan are onto something here. "Reputation equity" is the slack someone is willing to cut you or the business when you make a mistake. The greater your reputation equity, the more you can screw up without being destroyed. The lower your reputation equity, the more likely you are to be hammered when you do screw up. And because organizations are made up of human beings, we inevitably screw up at some point.

Okay, if reputation is an asset, just how much is it worth? If your entire business depends on trust, it may be worth the entire company. Even before Enron's spectacular collapse, Arthur Andersen had been caught red-handed massaging the financial reports of its clients. Apparently, the company placed profit before reputation despite the fact that its reputation was its principal asset. Once it lost its reputation in the Enron debacle, clients left in droves and the firm collapsed.

Fortunately, most reputation issues are not as dramatic. In 2005, United Technologies Corp. became concerned after surveys showed that most investors viewed the corporation as a sleepy Northeast company. Management asked Communications Consulting Worldwide to study how public perceptions affect a company's stock price. CCW, led by sociologist Pamela Cohen and former Ernst & Young strategist Jonathan Low, spent months building an elaborate computer model using data United Technologies had amassed over the years: studies tracking consumer perceptions of its brands, employee satisfaction, views of stock analysts and investors, corporate press releases, thousands of newspaper and magazine articles, and two years' worth of UTC financial information and daily stock movements. In the end, Cohen and Low concluded that 27 percent of UTC's stock market value was attributable to intangibles like its reputation.[4]

As one result of this reputation study, United Technologies initiated a new advertising campaign to promote its reputation in mid-2006. Did it make any difference? While no doubt other factors were at play, UTC's stock price did rise 21 percent between June 1, 2006 and December 31, 2007. So, as always, reputation is important, and you may be able to put a dollar value on it. What's new?

## Your Digital Rep

What's changed are the opportunities and challenges of managing reputation equity in a world without borders, thanks to the immediacy and reach of digitization. The explosion of social networks, e-communities, and the blogosphere are dramatically transforming the communications landscape. In this digitally flat world, one furious blogger can damage your personal or company reputation as other bloggers and commentators spread the word. You can't afford to ignore the danger to your digital rep, as Chick Edwards found out the hard way.

The good news is that you can build and protect your digital rep by communicating directly with key stakeholders through online interaction rather than only through traditional channels—word-of-mouth, newspapers, magazines, and television. You have to let the world know what you think, what you believe, and what you do that makes a difference.

In the last 20 years, "interest in reputation, and the value it has been given by both business audiences and the general public, has grown immensely," says Dr. Leslie Gaines-Ross, chief reputation strategist for Weber Shandwick. "In fact, media coverage of reputation alone has increased 108 percent over the past five years. Reputation management is now considered a legitimate body of knowledge, with a number of emerging new disciplines, including reputation recovery. Also, the sheer number and severity of corporate falls from grace in the last few years—coupled with the emergence of revolutionary ways of transmitting information, influential microconstituencies, and widespread mistrust of business—have magnified the need for a viable framework for the repair and recovery of damaged company reputations."

One reason executives care so much about this topic is that they now recognize how hard it is to maintain a reputation (or, looking at it another way, how easy it is to lose one). Gaines-Ross was surprised at how many of *Fortune* magazine's most admired companies slipped in the rankings over time. More than half of the top-ranked American companies in 2002 were not as highly-ranked in their industries by 2007. "The figures are even more compelling when we examined the world's most admired companies—79 percent of industry leaders in 2002 were not most admired in 2007," she says. "Looking ahead, companies that lead their industry today have much less than a 50/50 chance of being most admired five years from now."[5]

## Roadmap for Reputation Management

In this digitally-flat World 2.0, doing nothing is not an option—unless you want someone else to define your digital rep for you. But what exactly should you do? Use Figure 1.1, the Reputation Management Process, as a roadmap for managing reputation equity.

Your first step is to determine who your key stakeholders are and what issues they care about. As important as the defining issues of the 21st century may be—poverty, education, health, economic development, globalization, the environment, corporate responsibility, and transparency—your stakeholders may be just as concerned about microissues unique to your company or community. So think local as well as global.

Also understand how stakeholders see your reputation in the context of the issues that matter the most to them. Do you have a sterling reputation when it comes to product quality but a tarnished reputation on environmental affairs? Remember, this is all about *their* perceptions. Chapter 2 outlines tools for monitoring and measuring your personal or company reputation and discusses how to apply the results to make content and distribution better, more effective, more engaging, and more useful.

Next, set priorities and objectives for managing your reputation. Issue by issue, what kind of reputation would you like to have among

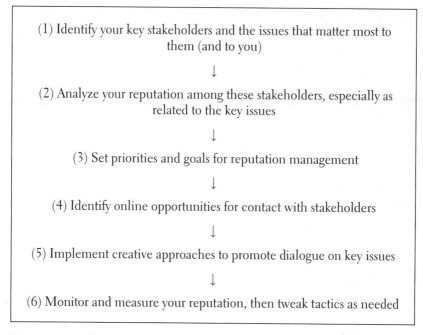

(1) Identify your key stakeholders and the issues that matter most to them (and to you)

↓

(2) Analyze your reputation among these stakeholders, especially as related to the key issues

↓

(3) Set priorities and goals for reputation management

↓

(4) Identify online opportunities for contact with stakeholders

↓

(5) Implement creative approaches to promote dialogue on key issues

↓

(6) Monitor and measure your reputation, then tweak tactics as needed

**Figure 1.1**    The Reputation Management Process

each stakeholder group? Where are the gaps between the reputation you desire and the reputation you actually have? Which issues and stakeholders are your top priorities?

Now you're ready to think about engaging, involving, and influencing your stakeholders. Chapter 3 introduces what I'm calling "the open source reputation," which is similar to the idea of open source computing: all participants contribute to creating your reputation. The open reputation requires specific strategies for engagement, content, building online environment, creating places, and distribution. In Chapter 4, I discuss particular strategies and tactics for engaging different stakeholders online to build and enhance reputation equity. Once you've got your engagement strategy and your content, what are your online opportunities for contacting stakeholders? Every organization has many communities with which it needs to work to build and manage reputation equity: customers, prospective customers, employees, vendors, stockholders, regulators, and so on. Chapter 5 describes ways to distribute your online content to the places where and when it will do the most good.

What are the new roles and new jobs companies need to implement an effective reputation management strategy? Who in your organization is going to be responsible for all of this? Chapter 6 outlines some ideas for the organizational requirements, including the possibility of naming a Chief Reputation Officer.

Chapters 7, 8, and 9 focus on your own reputation, earning digital reputation equity as a small business, and earning it as a substantial corporation. Thanks to Google and other search engines, strangers can assign you a reputation without your knowledge. If you are Chick Edwards, people will form one impression. If you are Warren Buffett, people will, it's fair to say, form another. Your reputation is your good name, and as you live these days, dropping nuggets of information as you go (a blog, an Amazon review, a court appearance, a letter to a magazine editor), someone can retrieve the nuggets easily to judge you as a potential employee, accountant, lawyer, consultant, or developer.

A small business may not be able to spend as much on earning, protecting, and defending its digital reputation as a major corporation, but it does not have to. The number of stakeholders is smaller, the business itself is less complex, and (generally) it does not have layers management and functional silos that can make earning a reputation a slog.

And while the principles of earning a digital reputation are the same whether you are an individual, running a small business, or the CEO of a large corporation, the CEO (generally) has resources the others do not. I will talk about the special problems all three face in Part III.

A new—and key—element in earning your digital reputation is the YouTube juggernaut. Chapter 10 discusses where it came from, where it is (it's the second largest search engine in the world—larger than Yahoo!), and how you can use it. Whether you own a local restaurant or pilot a multibillion dollar corporation, you have to be YouTube savvy.

It is not enough to proactively do things online to build reputation equity. The world being the nasty place that it can be, you must protect your digital rep on an ongoing basis and defend it when you or your company is under digital attack from negative comments, legitimate gripes, and slander. What can your investor relations people do online if they think Wall Street analysts are spreading negative rumors about your firm? What can a company do online to counter innuendos and lies about products, services, or policies? A crisis requires more than defending your reputation—you're facing an event that can potentially destroy it. What if the Immigration and Naturalization Service arrests 200 of your employees and closes your plant? What if your toys are found to be tainted with lead paint? What if a patron says she's found a human finger in your chili? Whether the crisis stems from external factors or an internal failure, Chapter 11 lays out digital steps you can take to minimize the damage to your reputation equity.

Even though reputation resides in the minds of your stakeholders, you have many opportunities online to get your news and views to stakeholders. However, as Chapter 12 explains, traditional public relations is giving way to a next-generation public affairs function for the digital environment. Who are the most influential or most-read bloggers—and therefore, where should you be placing content or commenting on content? What are the top e-communities—and where should you participate? What about product marketing and investor relations?

Arguably, the most effective effort to build a reputation using digital media was the Obama presidential campaign. Chapter 13 is a case study describing the campaign's online strategy for contacting supporters, recruiting volunteers, answering smears, and communicating the candidate's history and views—all of which contributed to a successful Election Day.

Chapter 14 looks at the future of reputation. Ultimately, what you do is more important than what you say. And here's where that idea of reputation as "money in the bank" comes into play. The best-managed companies can survive setbacks such as product recalls because its managers and employees have worked to earn a positive reputation over time. Stakeholders know the company is not in the habit of, say, selling lead-tainted toys. As I say in this chapter, trust and transparency go a long way toward protecting and rebuilding reputation equity.

So let's start with how you learn what people are saying about you behind your back.

# Psst—Want to Know Who's Talking About You?

I s somebody ratting on you? One night in February 2007, pedestrians passing a closed Taco Bell in New York City's Greenwich Village noticed activity inside the restaurant. More than 30 rats were racing around the restaurant's floors, playing with each other, and sniffing for food as they ran around tables and children's high chairs. In *Ratatouille* it was cute; in Taco Bell, it was disgusting. Someone called the local NBC-TV affiliate's tip line and they sent an independent news videographer to tape the bustle through a window.

The station ran the story on the early morning news. Even worse, the video quickly wound up on YouTube for the entire world to see. By the time Yum Brands, Taco Bell's parent, put out a public statement on its web page and on the media wires at 2:06 EST, the video had spread across the Internet and other TV stations had picked up the story. As David Vinjamuri, president of ThirdWay Brand Trainers, pointed out in his blog: "The seven hours that passed between the early-morning airing of the video on WNBC and WCBS and Taco Bell's response allowed the story to run nationally without any expression of regret from the company and made the whole mess look worse."

The mess wasn't helped, in my opinion, by Yum Brands' statement: "Nothing is more important to us than the health and safety of our customers. This is completely unacceptable and is an absolute violation of our high standards. We want to reassure customers that our restaurants are clean and safe. We will continue to work closely with the New York City Health Department, and if there's ever an issue we will immediately resolve it."

This sounds like something the company's public relations department and its lawyers would hammer out; an all-purpose apology that can be used for any of the corporation's 12,000 worldwide restaurants—just change the "New York City" reference and you're good to go. The company also did itself no favor by posting the response as a corporate statement rather than quoting a particular Yum Brands or Taco Bell executive. As I'll discuss in Chapter 11, when there's a crisis, the CEO or another C-level executive must be the organization's spokesperson.

A few rats in one franchisee's restaurant can pack a lot of pain for the brand, as Taco Bell found out. In the two weeks after the story broke, the stock of Yum Brands (KFC, Long John Silver's, Pizza Hut, A&W All American Food, and Taco Bell) fell more than 9 percent to $55.38 a share before it began to recover. In May 2007, Yum announced that it was closing the Greenwich Village Taco Bell plus nine others in New York. The video, however, lives on; when I Googled "Taco Bell and rats" not long ago, it was the first item that came up.[1]

## Early Warning System

While Yum Brands' sluggish response hurt its reputation, Comcast's quick response helped avoid a potential disaster. Michael Arrington, who owns TechCrunch, "a weblog dedicated to obsessively profiling and reviewing new Internet products and companies" and followed faithfully by something like 12,000 fans, was having trouble with his ISP. But let him tell the story:

"I called Comcast, and a recorded system said it would be back up in 30 minutes. That never happened. So I've been running around to various cafés and friend's houses to steal bandwidth and try to be online at least a little."

After 36 hours, "I called, waded through the automated system and a pitch to get a new premium cable company, and spoke to a real person. She told me that Comcast was having a California-wide outage and didn't know when it would be back up. I hung up on her mid-sentence. This California-wide outage seemed to be limited to my house—all of my friends said their Comcast connection was just fine. And then I lost my cool, tearing into Comcast on Twitter. Jeff Jarvis and others picked up the story and blogged about it.

"And this brings me to the point of this post. Within 20 minutes of my first Twitter message I got a call from a Comcast executive in Philadelphia who wanted to know how he could help. He said he monitors Twitter and blogs to get an understanding of what people are saying about Comcast, and so he saw the discussion break out around my messages. So Comcast sent a team out to fix my connection and apologized profusely."

Arrington pointed out that well before most organizations, Comcast has identified blogs—particularly Twitter—as an excellent early warning system to flag possible reputation challenges. He notes that it's ridiculously easy to do a brand search on Tweet Scan and create a feed for any new postings. "Whether you join in the conversation directly or reach out to aggrieved customers is up to you. But Twitter is the place where conversations are exploding well before they even make it to mainstream blogs. With the information just sitting there, it's surprising that more brands aren't watching the tweetosphere."[2]

## Always on Alert

It actually *is* ridiculously easy (and free) to set up a simple alert system. Of course, if you need something more sophisticated, a number of in-depth systems are available for a price. I'll talk about them in a minute.

To begin to see what people are saying about you, your company, your brand, your products, your industry, or all five, the simplest tool may be an alert from your favorite search site. Both Google and Yahoo! let you set up alerts so you're automatically notified when certain information—such as your name or your brand—shows up in search results. Google sends you an e-mail; Yahoo! will notify you by e-mail, instant message, pager, or cell phone.

For example, here's how Google Alerts work. Depending on how widely you want to cast your net, Google will notify you when it turns up new results from the latest news articles, web pages, blog posts, or videos that contain your search term. Google also has a Comprehensive alert, an aggregate of the latest results from multiple sources (News, Web, and Blogs), and a Groups alert that searches Google Groups (free opt-in groups of people with common interests).

To sign up, visit the Google Alerts home page (www.google.com/alerts), enter your search term, the type of alert you'd like (News, Web, Video, etc.), how often you'd like Google to check for results, and your e-mail address. When you're done, click the Create Alert button. Google sends a confirmation e-mail; you must click the link in that e-mail to activate your Alert.

You have one more alert decision to make: How often do you want Google to check for new results? The frequency you select determines how often Google checks for new results, not necessarily how often you'll receive alerts. If you select "once a day," Google checks for new results once a day, which means you'll get, at most, one e-mail per day if news or blogs or videos mention your search term. If you choose "as it happens," Google checks for new results continuously and sends an alert whenever it finds a new result.

Consider using alerts to:

- Stay up-to-date on your competitors, your industry, and key industry leaders.
- Follow a developing news story that affects your brand, your markets, your company, you, or all of the above.
- Watch for new videos on topics related to your company or career situation ("auto safety," "performance review," "job interview tips," or whatever you want to monitor).

The challenge here, as with virtually all Internet searches, is to come up with search terms that return relevant results. Too broad, and you get a haystack with the needle you want somewhere in the middle; too narrow, and you get just a few bits of straw. If your results are too broad, try more specific key words. Also try putting quotes around searches with multiple key words. If your search turns up nothing, try different key words, more general key words, fewer key words, or all three. Experiment to see what works for you.

## Listening for Tweets and More

Also consider setting up alerts on Twitter, a microblog site where users post "tweets" of up to 140 characters at a time. Even if you've never heard of Twitter, you can't afford to ignore what its 6 million-plus users are saying about you or your company. To set up Tweet Scan, which searches Twitter, the principles are the same as with Google Alerts. Go to the home page (www.tweetscan.com/alerts.php), click on the "Setup Email Alerts" button, and follow the directions. It's really that simple (and free).

Once you find particular blogs or web pages that you want to monitor regularly, check whether you can get updates via web feeds such as RSS. These web feeds deliver synopses to your e-mail address or to a news reader; then you can click through the link to read more.

Suppose you want to follow the latest *New York Times* business headlines. At the bottom of the newspaper's home page (www .nytimes.com), look for the orange RSS box. Click and you'll see a list of RSS feeds to which you can subscribe, such as business headlines or even a specific business topic such as media and advertising. Now click on that orange RSS box and you'll not only see the latest headlines, you can click to subscribe to the feed for that topic. If you're getting too much information, it's easy to unsubscribe.

Finally, here's a quick list of selected sites or services you may want to check out:

- Wikipedia – A free online encyclopedia written by volunteers. With more Wikipedia entries appearing by the day, you should know whether your company is mentioned and in what context. Another point: Wikipedia entries can be changed, updated, and corrected. www.wikipedia.org

- Digg – Users discover, submit, and vote on Internet content (blog posts, news stories, etc.) they like or think is important. Content that receives the most votes is featured higher on Digg's home page. You can subscribe to an RSS feed of the most popular Digg content. http://digg.com

- Delicious – This site invites users to bookmark their favorite or important web pages online, along with key words ("tags") to identify the content. You or anyone else can then search for all bookmarked pages according to content tags. It sounds complicated, but it's simple and also offers an RSS feed of the most popular bookmarks. http://delicious.com

- Boardreader – Many sites include forums or message boards where visitors can post comments, comment on other people's comments, and so on. Boardreader allows you to search forums, boards, image sites, and video sites by key word, language, date, relevancy, and other criteria. http://boardreader.com

## Technorati, Rapleaf, BlogPulse

Three more free tools you should know about are Technorati, Rapleaf, and BlogPulse. Technorati collects, highlights, and distributes the ongoing, online global blog conversation. Founder David Sifry says "as the leading blog search engine and most comprehensive source of information on the blogosphere, we index more than 1.5 million new blog posts in real time and introduce millions of readers to blog and social media content. Technorati Media extends our service and value by matching bloggers and social media creators with marketers who want to join the conversation."

Go to Technorati's search page (http://technorati.com/search), type your key words into the box, and click on the button. Your results come up in moments, organized by date, the most recent—which may be only minutes old—first.

Rapleaf (www.rapleaf.com) bills itself as a personal privacy service that allows users to look up their own information on the web as well as manage their reputation and privacy. The service is free to individuals; businesses and developers may have to pay a fee for the services.

Rapleaf collects demographic information such as name, age, gender, location, occupation, where you worked, what university you went to, and your first known Internet activity. It also automatically collects online communities and social networks with which an e-mail address is associated. It harvests this data from publicly available online sources such as blogs, newsgroups, social networks, message boards, forums, and so on.

When you check your own information, you can also see the source of the data. Because you know the source, you can take steps to correct any inaccuracies or update your information as needed.

BlogPulse (www.blogpulse.com), a service of Nielsen BuzzMetrics, says it is an automated trend discover system for blogs. It includes a search engine for blogs, tools to track daily blog activity on people, news stories, news sources, and more, and blogger profiles to identify blogs by activity and relative influence. BlogPulse is not a general search engine like Google or Yahoo!

Besides doing your own search on BlogPulse, the site offers a number of RSS feeds including top news stories, top news sources, top links (the most cited or most popular links appearing in blog entries daily), key people (those with the most citations on a given day), key phrases (an indication of the topics being blogged about that day), and more.

## DIY Tracking

Good as they are, free tools have their limitations. For one thing, you have to sift through all the results; if you harvest too many results, it becomes a full-time job just to click, read, and analyze them. Fee-based tools can offer more convenience and flexibility.

One example is Trackur, a do-it-yourself online reputation monitoring tool to which you can subscribe. You set up searches and the system automatically monitors the Web for key words that appear on news sites, blogs, and other social media. You can track your own

name, your company brands, industry trends, a competitor's news—
any key words you choose.

Trackur helps you stay on top of your digital rep by monitoring
many web channels and allowing you to save items, sort them, share
them via e-mail, and subscribe to an RSS feed. And you can run multiple searches, as often as every hour. However, Trackur can't distinguish
between positive and negative content. According to its web site,
"Sentiment analysis is notoriously difficult, and no company has mas-
tered an automated approach to it. For example, the phrase 'Apple's
iPhone is wicked bad' would cause headaches for even Google!"

## Hiring Professional Help

Another choice for professional help is Radian6, which CEO Marcel
LeBrun describes as an online listening and engagement tool. "We
monitor the entire social web, from blogs and videos to microblogs
like Twitter and more, into one place," Marcel tells me, "so it allows
you to track what people are saying automatically. It allows you to
analyze the conversations to make sense of what's being said, and it
helps you engage and participate in the conversation to understand as
well as measure the results."

For example, a large corporation might find 3,500 conversations
a day that mention the company and its brand. This is a form of
the haystack problem: which ones should you pay attention to first?
Which are the most important for your reputation? Which are the
most engaged, passionate conversations as opposed to passing mentions? Which blogs, news stories, or videos are people paying the most
attention to? Which conversations have the most influence on your
reputation? And perhaps most importantly, which conversations are
originating from your customers who are expecting a response?

Marcel tells me that when he talks to business executives about
how tools like Radian6 can meet their needs, two kinds of questions
come up. The first category is from the few executives who still wonder what the social web is and why it's relevant to the way they have
always done business. The answer depends on how game-changing

World 2.0 is for your organization and how critical is it for you to engage with your stakeholders—and interested outsiders—who have the most influence on your reputation.

The second category of questions is from executives who already understand that World 2.0 has changed the game. These managers know they should cover online conversations, but need advice about how to best listen and participate in these conversations. Marcel's answer is to set up a broad "field of listening." He notes that "online video is growing in importance; your reputation is not affected just by blogs any more. Blogs are only one part of the conversation. For that reason, we cover everything—blogs, images, videos, microblogging content, and social networks."

World 2.0 has really enabled an entirely new multi-purpose communications medium which LeBrun dubs "the social phone" since customers can now call out to your company from whatever social platform they are using. He concludes, "Your business needs to learn how to appropriately answer the social phone." It is as important now as any other communications medium.

## Influence and Overlap

One more fee-based service I want to mention is TNS Cymfony, which tracks and aggregates both traditional and social media influences. Jim Nail, the chief strategy and marketing officer, explains that different sources of information—individually and in combination—can influence people's perceptions of a brand or firm at different times. "Traditional media has grown more fragmented while social media has grown in importance," he says. "We look at the number of points of influence plus the overlapping, intersecting ways that each of those sources influence each other. Our analysis challenge is enormously complex because different combinations influence consumers differently."

To know what consumers really think about your organization, you have to be able to understand and interpret these very intricate interactions. Cymfony's approach involves a three-step process. Step one is retrieving all of the raw material relevant to a particular client, using Cymfony's own spiders, crawlers, robots, and more. Cymfony marries that material with feeds from other content partners and cleans it up so the result is coherent, client-focused content.

Step two sends that material through Cymfony's natural language processing engine. Basically, the technology breaks paragraphs into sentences and sentences into parts of speech to understand the topics being talked about. What adjectives are being used and is the tone positive or negative? How are the conversations changing over time?

Step three puts this analysis together with advertising expenditure data and consumer research results. This multifaceted approach allows Cymfony to dissect the many sources and consequences of market influence for each client—and determine where, when, and how to most effectively influence the target audience.

One problem Cymfony sees more often (one that World 2.0 has aggravated) is the "I-think-people-might-be-saying-nasty-things-about-my-company-but-I-don't-know-what-they're-saying" problem. Managers don't know whether people are saying nasty things, exactly how nasty they're being, and whether they should be worried. Jim notes that you can only know if you examine as much content as possible and carefully analyze the material to classify the positive and the negative.

## Travelocity's Moment of Truth

Have you heard the story of Travelocity's zero fare to Fiji? It's been a few years but it still shows up on blogs now and then. The online travel site faced a tough call when a sharp-eyed frequent flier noticed that Travelocity had mistakenly posted a $0 fare from Los Angeles to Fiji (plus $51 in taxes). It took just a few minutes for word of this super-bargain to spread across the Internet—and hundreds of people clicked to buy.

At the time, Travelocity was readying a new branding campaign to highlight the company's customer service commitment. "One of the tenets was we're going to make mistakes," CEO Michelle Peluso told *Business Week*. "What we really have to figure out is, are we going to walk the walk?"

Travelocity noticed the Fiji activity immediately. Although the fare error was clearly unintentional, it gave Peluso the opportunity to show what Travelocity stood for. After a lot of internal discussion, the CEO not only honored the fare, she joined the online discussion to wish the fliers a fun flight. "It cost us money," Peluso recalls. "And it was frustrating because we knew people knew it was a fake fare. But it made us a stronger company and cemented our relationships with our suppliers."

The price tag was $2 million, but the upward bounce to Travelocity's reputation was, as they say, priceless.[3]

## Now What?

Once you've classified the material, you can focus on the negative. What are people saying that's negative? Where is it coming from? How negative is it? Is it starting to cross over from social media, or even from small blogs? Is it starting to seep into the more professional media company blogs? Is it starting to spread across the social networks? Does it jump to traditional media?

With the tools I've described, you can not only monitor what people are saying about you, you can see how people react to your response when you address the negative issues. Are people buying your story? Are they buying your answer? Are they raising new objections or new questions? Are you slowing or stopping the spread of negatives? Remember, this is an ongoing process, not a one-time fix.

The other thing you can do once you know what people are saying about you is to identify them and their relationship to the organization. These are Steps 1 and 2 in the Reputation Management Process I showed you in Chapter 1. How significant is an individual blogger? (If he's Michael Arrington and you're Comcast, the answer is "very.") Is the issue one that will affect customers directly? Shareholders? Employees? How will what you're hearing be likely to influence your reputation among stakeholders?

Now that you know what people are saying about you, what can you do to build your reputation . . . or minimize the nasty things they're saying?

# Shape Your Reputation

# Building Reputation: Start a Dialogue

I n the summer of 2006, Paul Levy read in *The New York Times* that few *Fortune* 500 CEOs have blogs. His first thought was: "I'm not a *Fortune* 500 CEO, but I run a billion-dollar business and I *am* a CEO. I should start one and see what happens."

Paul is CEO of the Beth Israel Deaconess Medical Center in Boston, which has a teaching affiliation with Harvard Medical School. He had been Harvard Medical School's executive dean for administration, but this was his first time in hospital administration. As CEO, he had been learning fascinating things about hospitals and the medical field. He began blogging because, he tells me, "I thought people would want to hear about all the interesting things going on in medicine and healthcare."

## Transparency and Trust

Although few healthcare executives will talk as openly about medical concerns, technology, and treatment, Paul embraces transparency, as you can see on his blog (http://runningahospital.blogspot.com). Members of the medical profession may shy away from such discussions and disclosures because they fear being judged by the public.

Paul's view is "you are going to get judged anyway. Isn't it better to state your point of view and create a framework for the discussion, rather than just being attacked?"

What about the legal department's strictures? Not a problem. Paul tells me that the Dana Farber Cancer Institute, which also believes in transparency, has found that "if you are actually honest with patients and families, and disclose early and often, your chance of being sued seems to be less. The reason is not hard to understand. People fundamentally trust their doctors and their caregivers. If they don't, they go elsewhere."

In fact, Paul says Beth Israel and Dana Farber have found that transparency builds trust: "If someone who has cared for you over several years says, 'I am really sorry to tell you this, but I just made a mistake, and I may have caused you harm,' people will say, 'Thank you for telling me. I understand the risks of medical care and I trust you even more for having told me the bad news.' The other side of it is, even if you don't disclose it to the patients, a mistake is discoverable in a lawsuit anyway. So who are you hiding it from?"

But what about the time it takes to blog? Couldn't the chief executive officer find a better use of his time?

Paul tells me: "There are lots of parts to the job of a CEO, but one of them is, in the crassest possible terms, to position your company in the best possible light in the public environment; among your consumers, potential consumers, and potential adversaries. What better way to do that than to write when you want, about the topics you want, in your own words? You're not being edited by reporters or anyone else; you can get your message out in thirty seconds, and the whole world can see what you've said."

Not only is blogging a good way for Paul to speak out, it's a good way to get a dialogue going and to learn from the response—both positive and negative. "Sometimes you don't like what people write," he points out. "But they're saying it about you anyway, and isn't it better to hear it directly? So I view this as part of the CEO's responsibility to use these media, just as you used to use television, radio, and newspapers—and perhaps more so. Those other media often aren't as effective, particularly among certain audience groups."

# Open Source Reputation

Paul Levy keeps up a steady blog dialogue with an unusually complex constituency. Beth Israel Deaconess's stakeholders include patients and their families, insurers, policy-makers, government officials, administrators, and nearly 8,000 physicians, nurses, and nonclinical employees. If you read his blog and the comments, you'll see the give and take between and among his readers. And the comments come from all over the world, not just Boston—Asia, Africa, Australia, New Zealand, and South America. The result is what I call "the open source reputation."

The open source reputation is similar to the idea of open source computing. All of your stakeholders contribute to creating your reputation. Although you can provide some direction and have some influence, you can't control what people say about you (in fact, you never could, but now they can say it in exceedingly public forums). That's why you must plan for engaging different stakeholders online to build and enhance your reputation equity.

Because of the impact of mobile devices—cell phones, Internet access, and e-mail—managing your reputation is like running a 24-hour gas station with pumps in every country. To understand and shape your open source reputation, you need to be aware of what's happening on the Web and the effect on your stakeholders (as I explained in Chapter 2).

Another important point is that the Web is becoming emotive: the combination of visuals and everything else on the screen provokes a reaction or inspires passion from people or groups. This determines where you—and all web users—decide to click when you go online and where you choose to engage in dialogue.

If you're like me, you have a regular routine of visiting the digital environments that are most meaningful to you. You might visit eight sites daily—for example, LATimes.com, CNN.com, Facebook, LinkedIn, *The Huffington Post*, and a few favorite blogs. You may look once or twice a week at sites related to your hobby, whether it's wine collecting, cars, gardening, or woodworking. You might be fanatical about checking a favorite sports site (Red Sox, Yankees, Steelers, ice skating), and look at certain shopping sites and health sites fairly regularly. And, if you're like me, you keep the dialogue going as often as you can by responding to articles or blog posts on the sites you visit.

Your organization should have an online routine, as well. Once you begin monitoring what people are saying about you, your company, and your brand and you've identified the most influential sites or blogs, you should visit them regularly, look for new voices, look for other sites that are currently, or should be, important to the company.

It's not enough to simply visit—you have to pay close attention to what's being said and join the conversations to keep the dialogue going. Paul Levy says that he regularly visits Geekdoctor.blogspot .com, KevinMD.com, and http://healthaffairs.org/blog/, all of which (and more) you can find linked to his blog. This is part of how he keeps the dialogue going, in addition to reading and responding to comments posted on his blog.

## What Do You Stand For?

You and your company can now say "Here is what I stand for" in a way you never could before. You can do it through blogs; web sites like Facebook, LinkedIn, and MySpace; videos on YouTube and Flickr; on Twitter, and on your own web site(s). You can visit other digital neighborhoods, introduce yourself, and participate in the community life. The more you do the more reputation equity you tend to build.

I can't say it too often: Reputation counts because people have so many choices today. If you want a cup of coffee, you can go to the Mobil Mart, Starbucks, Dunkin' Donuts, McDonald's, or the local deli. It's the same thing in World 2.0. If you want to buy a dress shirt, you can go to Overstock.com, LLBean.com, Brooksbrothers.com, Bestcustomshirt.com, and dozens—perhaps hundreds—of other sites. (A Google search of "buy dress shirt" turned up almost 2,500 results.) Where do you go?

If you don't already have a favorite in mind, or if you want to try something new, you might try sites you've heard about from friends or colleagues. Or you might follow up on a site you saw mentioned on someone's Facebook page as "the best place to buy a shirt." Or you might post a note on someone's blog asking, "What's been your experience with Overstock.com?" "With Zappos?" "With Blue Nile?" All of these dialogues build on each other and contribute to the company's open source reputation.

It's relatively easy for companies to establish dialogues with obvious stakeholders such as customers, employees, and shareholders. The firm can identify them, see what they're saying, and react. It may be more difficult to start a dialogue with other groups like vendors, regulators, and prospective customers.

I recommend that companies establish separate environments for different discussions. In other words, you should start a dialogue specifically with employees, one specifically with vendors, and another with your best, most enthusiastic customers. You might password-protect some sites where these dialogues take place (such as conversations with vendors) while having others open to all. In fact, it might very well be to the company's benefit if someone—a stock analyst, a prospective customer, a state legislator—can see what the CEO is saying to employees. The better sites are going to continue to be a mix of user-generated and enterprise-generated content. That's what keeps visitors coming back, keeps them interested, and keeps the discussions moving.

I recommend that organizations create a constituency map: customers, employees, vendors. Or: patients, physicians, pharmaceutical companies, insurers. Or: shareholders, analysts, regulators. Because different constituencies are interested in different aspects of the organization, management's task is to create compelling content for and with each constituency. This is your chance to let each constituency know exactly what you stand for.

The deeper idea of an open source reputation is that the stronger the dialogue, the stronger the relationship and the more reputation equity you build. You become the shirt shop of choice, the restaurant of choice. Customers (and other constituents) want to go where, as the *Cheers* theme said, everybody knows their name. And you'll have banked some goodwill to draw on if and when something unexpectedly happens.

## Will You Join Us?

It's never too early to get a dialogue going. Months before gasoline prices began soaring to stratospheric levels—in July 2005, to be exact—Chevron Corporation established a web site to start a dialogue around energy (http://willyoujoinus.com). Years later, the site is still going strong.

Helen Clark, the head of corporate marketing at Chevron, tells me that the effort started in 2004. The global policy and regulatory environment in which the corporation operates is critical to its ability to produce energy. Its environment is shaped by how regulators and others view the industry and its importance. If regulators understand the supply and demand situation they can make informed decisions when creating policy or regulations or giving a company the ability to find oil. Much of Chevron's campaign for the last three years, says Helen, has been focused on education and engagement, so the people involved in the decision-making can make an informed decision.

But back when it was researching the issue, Chevron found that the influential policy-makers felt the energy industry was not taking part in the conversation. Helen says, "People were talking about supply and demand issues; they were talking about energy efficiency, they were talking about the role of energy companies, but energy companies were not really engaged in that discussion."

Although Chevron makes it clear that it supports the willyou joinus site, the corporation is not pushing a point of view. "When we set up the debate," says Helen, "we always have two experts who have opposing views on this subject. We commission them, but we do not edit them. We give them full editorial right. As you can imagine, that's giving up a lot of control for any corporation, which was hotly debated at the time, but we wanted to set this up as a real place where the community could listen to experts, learn more, and comment."

Willyoujoinus invites visitors to share ideas about energy-related issues. The site's first question, "How can we make oil and gas supplies last longer, as the search for other fuels continues?" provoked 1,072 responses from 689 people who registered on the site. Other questions have included, "How should we expand our energy conservation efforts?" "Can countries be energy independent or should they plan for interdependency as the way of the future?" and "Can biofuels play a more significant role in the world's portfolio of energy resources?"

As I write this, the topic under discussion is: "In a world where we need all the energy we can find to meet growing demand, how do we do more with less? What are the best methods for encouraging participation among individuals, organizations, and governments to reduce overall consumption, and use our current energy supply more wisely? How might these efforts help address concerns about global climate change?"

Not everyone, of course, is enthusiastic about the site or the dialogue. Njoel commented: "I have not been here for a while and in my absence . . . nothing has changed, advanced, or moved. The discussions are the same, the questions are the same, and the answers are as obscure as ever. I ask the host what are the latest events that move the energy crisis into new directions. What is the status of hydrogen in the overall scheme of total energy independence?"

To which a Roy Johnston responded, "We need to get away from monocultures and get back to mixed farming, with synergetic interactions between tillage, livestock and horticulture, in a managed system with as much added value as possible on products transported to market. This could be done by a co-operative arrangement between a cluster of farms. Such a system could include energy production, by managing the development of the hedgerows surrounding the fields, extending them with parallel strips of coppice, to be harvested for wood-chips for the energy market, on a short rotation cycle. Strip forestry surrounding fields would also supply shelter, increasing the productivity of the enclosed fields. . . ."

Not unexpectedly, different topics stimulated different response levels. Once the responses seem to peter out, Chevron hires an independent outsider, The Aspen Institute, to analyze and prepare a white paper on the discussion for anyone to download and print. These, like the entire discussion, remain on the site.

Helen says that the site has had over 3.5 million visitors over the past couple years. More than half come from outside the United States, and Chevron's tracking research found that 80 percent of the users agreed the site was valuable, and 64 percent said it was very or extremely valuable. "I think originally we thought a lot of people would go back to take part in the debate, but we found that over 60 percent of people who use the site frequently go back just to hear what other people are saying. So there is this kind of voyeur piece of it also." Chevron also found that half the people who go to the site want to learn more about the issues, so they go to the issues section. The tracking survey found the users saying resoundingly that they liked the site, want to go there, and like to find out what's there.

While the site is remarkably open to the diverse philosophies it hopes to attract, it does have guidelines: "Submissions may be edited to meet the Community Guidelines, or for grammar, spelling and length. Every effort is made to retain the original meaning of all edited submissions. Please review the Community Guidelines again to see why your submission may have been edited. If you still disagree with the edits, please visit the Contact Us page." Chevron's Community Guidelines seem so reasonable that I've reproduced them in full (Figure 3.1).

I asked Helen what, if anything, Chevron might recommend to another corporation that it is thinking of setting up a site to engage and educate an audience. She says that management believes one thing that helped willyoujoinus be successful is that it doesn't try to push Chevron's point of view to create a community. She thinks the online community—more than any other community—is harsh on someone if they see you are pushing your own agenda while pretending to do something else. "If you are honestly trying to set up a forum for discussion, then you need to be open and honest and do it. Not have a kind of subplot or another agenda, because the community will see right through it. I think that was one thing that we tried very hard at and I think it has been successful." At the same time, of course, the corporation pushes its agenda at Chevron.com, says Helen, because that's the place to do it.

She says that while they would not do a lot differently if they were starting again, they would begin with a different mindset. "Three years ago it felt kind of scary. We didn't quite know what would happen.

To participate in the discussion, users must complete a simple registration, sign in, and comply with the following guidelines:

- Address the specific topic of the discussion.
- Support your point of view with well-founded arguments and facts.
- Identify yourself by name, unless doing so will compromise your personal security or livelihood, or that of others.
- Respect the views of others and consider them carefully before responding with a posting of your own.

Members may not submit content that:

- is threatening, abusive, libelous, indecent, or graphic, including hate speech directed at a specific ethnic group, nationality, sexual orientation, organization, corporation, religion, and so on?
- infringes on copyright protections
- attempts to disguise the origin of the posting
- impersonates an individual or misrepresents a relationship with any person or organization
- encourages others to commit illegal acts or to harass individuals
- advertises or promotes goods and services
- using the site to attempt to influence voting on a particular bill, or proposition

In addition, the following types of postings are not permitted:

- messages that are not relevant to the debate topic
- repetitive messages, including cross-posting, flooding, and spamming
- messages of excessive length (more than 1,000 words or 2,500 characters)
- messages with no content
- viruses, files, or code which might interrupt, destroy, or limit functionality of the site or any computer software or equipment

**Figure 3.1** Chevron's Community Discussion Guidelines
*Source:* http://willyoujoinus.com/discussion/guidelines/

We didn't know whether people would come, what the discussion would be like. We didn't know whether people would look at it positively or negatively. You have to be willing to relinquish a little bit of control. It's different from a print ad where you can just print it and it is what it is."

## Zappos: Reputation = Brand

Here's another example, this time from the world of online retailing. Tony Hsieh, the founder and CEO of Zappos, sees "reputation" as another word for "brand." In an e-mail exchange with me, he emphasized that "We definitely think about the Zappos brand every day. We want the Zappos brand to be about the very best customer service and customer experience."

He then made an interesting point: "Our #1 priority is actually not customer service. Our #1 priority is company culture. Our belief is that if you get the culture right, most of the other stuff, like great customer service and a great long-term brand, will just fall into place naturally on its own. In fact, we believe that a company's culture and a company's brand (or reputation) are really just two sides of the same coin."

Zappos formalized the definition of the company culture with ten core values:

1. Deliver WOW through service.
2. Embrace and drive change.
3. Create fun and a little weirdness.
4. Be adventurous, creative, and open-minded.
5. Pursue growth and learning.
6. Build open and honest relationships with communication.
7. Build a positive team and family spirit.
8. Do more with less.
9. Be passionate and determined.
10. Be humble.

Tony says, "We hire people based on those core values, and will fire people if they're not living up to the core values. By making sure that our employees exude the core values, we create a consistent reputation with our customers, vendors, and employees. Because we hire for culture, when customers call our Customer Loyalty Team (call center), they are talking to someone who is genuinely passionate about delivering great service. We don't have scripts, and every rep is empowered to take care of our customers. As unsexy and low-tech as it may sound, we believe that the telephone is actually one of the best branding devices out there, because we have the customer's undivided attention for 5–10 minutes, and customers can get a feel for our culture through the phone."

In addition to phone contact, Zappos uses Twitter to build a dialogue with customers as well as internal audiences (see http://twitter .zappos.com/employees). Tony says, "We have hundreds of Zappos employees on Twitter and have aggregated all of our employee tweets. We've found that Twitter allows us to make a more personal connection to both our employees and our customers. It makes the relationship a lot more personal, which is what we ultimately want people to feel about Zappos." No nameless, faceless corporate monolith here—every tweet enhances Zappos' reputation as a corporation of authentic, people-oriented people.

## A Twitter Moment

Because Twitter is such an immediate way to start a dialogue—Zappos, JetBlue, H&R Block, Dell, TurboTax, and Comcast are among the many firms that monitor Twitter—and because it has been growing like Topsy (over 3.2 million accounts by October 2008, two years after its launch), let me take a moment to walk you through a Twitter experience.

Go to www.Twitter.com and get started by creating a username and password. (You can also watch a short video about Twitter, which is a little less than a blog and a little more than no contact.) Once you've set up your account, you can start posting your own tweets and follow those of friends, acquaintances, and even strangers. Twitter also works on mobile phones, where the 140-character limit means you can send and receive messages via text messaging. If you like, you can send tweets via e-mail.

Maybe your initial reaction to Twitter may be a heartfelt, "Who cares if you're making coffee . . . cooking eggs . . . getting in the car . . . stuck in traffic again." But tweets can actually contain valuable nuggets if you listen carefully. Recent JetBlue-related tweets included, "Nice plugin stations at the JetBlue terminal, touch screen ordering menu at each seat as well." "The food court at jetblue's new terminal is all touch screen ordering, what a pain in the ass." "Any chance of Boston to Kansas City flight in near future? Midwest is the only airline that does direct these days." "JetBlue is the best airline I've ever been on. It's domestic service is better than international flights I've been on."

Since all these tweets are public, it is possible for someone at JetBlue to ask for more information from the Twitterer who thought the touch screen ordering was a pain in the ass. What was the problem? How could the experience be improved? And, of course, it can thank people for their compliments.

Now that you've started the dialogue, you have to give people something to talk about.

# Building Reputation: Something to Talk About

N ike+ (nikeplus.com) has, as they say, got legs. It's more than a brand-based site—it's a full-blown social network built around runners. It's not like Nike's losing the market-share race over running shoes—in fact, it's the dominant force, with some 60 percent of the U.S. market. Its problem was that it only had about a 10 percent share of serious runners, who typically buy their shoes in specialty running shops. To build its reputation among those customers, it introduced Nike+, which involves a line of shoes, a custom-built chip, the web site, and the customer's own Apple iPod nano.

"Nike Plus is not just another product aimed at improving the cushioning of the footwear," said Matt Powel, an analyst at Sport-ScanInfo, an athletic-footwear research firm. "It gets at improving the experience for the runner, at building the community." It gives Nike—and runners—something to talk about.

If you've never tried the Nike+ iPod Sport Kit system, here's how it works. You put a tiny sensor inside your Nike+ running shoe (identified by the Swoosh and "+" sign) and plug a small receiver into your iPod nano. As you run, the sensor broadcasts the speed, distance, and calories burned to the receiver. You can check these figures on the nano's screen even as you listen to your music.

Nike has struck a chord with runners, selling 1.3 million Nike+ iPod Sport Kits in the first two years. It has also sold 500,000 Nike+ Sport Bands, a wrist-watch device which functions like the nano for runners who don't want to listen to music as they jog along.

It's the community aspect of Nike+ that really gives people something to talk about. Back home, runners can upload their data to the nikeplus.com web site and map their runs, challenge other participants, form marathon teams, let friends track their progress, and more. Last August, for example, 800,000 runners logged on and signed up to run a 10K race sponsored by Nike simultaneously in 25 cities, from Chicago to São Paulo. Today, the site is a virtual gathering place where runners collectively have logged more than 100 million miles. Clearly, Nike has built up a serious lead in World 2.0 by setting up an online community for everyone who runs.[1]

## It's All About the Experience . . .

The best web destinations are "places," designed to offer an experience rather than static, text-heavy sites. They offer news, information, entertainment, or, as Nike+ has done, a place where people with similar interests can swap stories. They also give other sites (blogs, news sites, Twitter users, YouTube fans) something to "talk" about.

How do you do this? How do you design an experience? How do you provide appropriate content for customers and other stakeholders . . . and how does this affect your reputation equity?

You don't do it with static, text-heavy sites or pages. Experience includes sizzle (sight, sound, etc.) as well as content and user-friendly functionality (if appropriate, put the fun in functionality). Keep it simple. Make it quick and easy for visitors to listen to a podcast, view a webcast, comment on a blog post. People will go to—and stay with—the destination they think offers the best experience, the one that has the best reputation.

You and your company don't have to come up with all the content. The experience can and should be a digital community, an online place where visitors can listen to you and to each other, to connect by asking questions and sharing ideas. That's what makes Nike+ so appealing to its visitors—the opportunity to share their successes, challenge each other, hear about upcoming races, and more.

Don't forget to include links to content and resources that complement your site's content and that provide more info on the topics visitors care most about (issues you identified as important in Step 1 of Figure 1.1). This is part of the open-source reputation. Link to news stories on reputable blogs such as BlogHer or *The Huffington Post,* for instance. Or link to YouTube videos or Flickr photos. (As I mentioned back in Chapter 2, part of your goal is to get to know your stakeholders and what they think of you, so be sure to monitor content provided by your visitors.)

AlwaysOn, a media company that tracks venture capital in digital entertainment and related fields, wants its online destination to reflect the market it serves. Tony Perkins, founder and editor, says that 90 percent of the site's content comes from members of the AlwaysOn community. Its audiences are cutting-edge, so its sites are cutting-edge, with lots of video material, for example, along with an open-source video player. It regularly adds new resources to enhance the experience by allowing visitors to make the most of the content they care about the most.

Tony tells me, "Our marketing philosophy is what I call pursuing the art of attraction versus promotion. That means to deliver quality products and services. Through that we attract and build our brand. Obviously we reach out with e-mail, which is our number one form of marketing. We do research on the markets, so we call up law firms and speakers and interview people in the marketplace. It's a business-to-business market, so it's more easily identifiable than a broader consumer market."

But what else can an organization do to engage stakeholders? At AlwaysOn.goingon.com, "we don't think of our readers in a traditional media sense, as our subscribers," says Tony, who as founder of *Red Herring* magazine knows something about subscribers. "We think of them as members to our community. We have a set of what we call sub-brands—GoingGreen, OnMedia, OnHollywood, VC&$. Everything on the site is color-coordinated with those sub-brands.

We also create a personality around the brand that reflects the market we serve—an edgy, entrepreneurial cutting-edge site. It all makes us part of the community we serve." And that personality, of course, is part of creating AlwaysOn's reputation.

## Earn Their Respect

Polish your digital rep by respecting your community's privacy. You want to be able to "listen" to what visitors are saying about you and your organization. You also want visitors to trust that you won't misuse their comments and data. And you want your content to be trustworthy. Keep your content free of abuse and spam. Fight the urge to post prepackaged messages that are essentially company propaganda, says Owen Thomas, managing editor of Valleywag, a Silicon Valley gossip site. Instead, he tells me, "there's an opportunity to make an impression by actually being bluntly honest." When you involve your employees in the experience, the way Zappos showcases tweets from its people, you risk airing some of your dirty laundry. "To get the benefit, you have to take that risk," Thomas says. "If that stuff isn't coming out, then no one is going to believe any of the positive things that are being said."

As an example of how to tarnish your digital rep—to get people talking about you in a negative way—consider this example (which I've masked) from a blog titled Online Reputation Handbook. As part of a blog, an employee of XYZ Financial Advisors wrote a 410-word post that defended the company ("all of the advisors I've worked with are honest") and the industry ("There is absolutely NOTHING at all wrong with selling financial products or services."). The blogger concluded: "XYZ Financial is a top-notch financial services company with more than 10,000 advisors providing personal financial service to more than 2 million clients. The VAST majority of those clients are very satisfied with the service they receive, and the overwhelming majority of financial advisors are VERY trustworthy, capable, dedicated, and happy to be working with a forward-thinking company like XYZ Financial."

The post's critics jumped on this with both feet. The post is too long, too well written, used excessive CAPITAL LETTERS, employed vague wording, and, most damning of all, that last paragraph sounded like corporate-speak.[2] Better to say nothing than be suspected of being a corporate mouthpiece.

## Give 'Em Something to Talk About

Dan Gillmor, founder and director of the Knight Center for Digital Media Entrepreneurship at Arizona State University's Cronkite School, reminds me that "People will talk about what you're doing whether or not you give them a place to do it, whether or not you're paying attention to what they say. It's important to participate in that conversation." Companies with blogs, he says, tend to be more connected to their constituencies than companies without blogs. In other words, they're going to talk about you anyway, so give them real, reputation-enhancing content to talk about and a destination to keep the dialogue going.

Companies with blogs may be more connected to their constituencies, but a recent Forrester report said that only one in six consumers trusts company blogs. That ranks lower than every other form of content Forrester's researchers asked about, including broadcast and print media, direct mail, and e-mail from companies. In reporting the findings, Forrester's Josh Bernoff pointed out that "like any other marketing channel, blogging can work. *But it's not about you; it's about your customer.*"

Bernoff's advice: Blog about the customer's problem. Blog to your hordes of fans. Blog about issues at the core of the community. Blog because you're a celebrity (Jeff Bezos, Donald Trump, Oprah Winfrey), and if you're selling to businesses, get your employees in on the act.[3]

I recommend that you and your people react to comments that people leave on your site and respond to reporters or consumer advocates who contact you. This beefs up your content, makes commenters feel welcome and appreciated, and gives people even more to talk about. Also reach out by posting comments and content on important blog sites and other destinations frequented by your key stakeholders. You want to connect with your audience wherever they like to click, and show them that you care about what they care about. (YouTube is such an important destination it has its own chapter later in the book.)

## Beyond Official Media

There was a time when people dreamed of or dreaded seeing their name in the local newspaper (or on the cover of *Rolling Stone*). Your reputation was really on the line when you made the front page. But how much do traditional newspapers or news magazines (like *Time* and *Newsweek*) matter in today's wired world? In World 2.0, how will reputation be shaped by official news media outlets versus online output of citizen journalists (who may be bloggers, Twitterers, or YouTube posters)?

In World 2.0, people often pay as much attention to the opinions of reviewers who post on Amazon.com as they do to the reviewers who write for media such as *The New York Times*. So what if citizen journalists aren't professionally trained and their comments aren't professionally edited? Think about the thousands of people who buy Zagat guides or check Yelp.com (www.yelp.com) to see what ordinary people say about local restaurants before they make reservations. It seems to be the age of reputation power to the people.

To find out more about the future of professional journalism—and what it means for personal and corporate reputations—I talked with Dan Gillmor, because he was one of the first journalists to comment at length on such issues (he's the author of *We the Media*). Today, he tells me, many different trends are working at once, "but there is going to be a much more diverse and, I hope, more useful ecosystem developing where people who had only been an audience will be part of the journalism. It's a very messy period with more information and— once we figure out how to sort it and identify the quality stuff—better information."

At best, Dan sees a murky future for newspapers. *The Christian Science Monitor* has abandoned its print edition and The Tribune Company, which owns the *Chicago Tribune*, the *Los Angeles Times*, and other papers, has filed for bankruptcy. Denver's *Rocky Mountain Times* has gone out of business. "What newspapers do, I hope, will be preserved, though there is plenty of evidence that a lot of what newspapers do is going to go away for the medium term. The 'monopoly' model has been broken." In other words, newspapers (and television) are no longer the primary source of news for a growing number of people. Most of Dan's students at Arizona State don't buy newspapers or read the paper versions, nor do the younger people in my office. But they do read newspaper articles online.

Dan makes another good point: Newspapers are wide and shallow except during periods of national trauma, when they dive deeply into the issues. But as a rule, they're not deep because they can't be everything to everyone. When they do their job well, they reflect the community's values, problems, and possibilities. "But even there, they've almost never reflected the entire community's reality, because—especially today—most newspapers have written off the bottom 60 percent of the economic demographic because they're not the people the advertisers want to reach."

Yet while newspapers are suffering, online journalism is booming, in part because citizen reporters only need a computer and a free blog to begin filing stories. Still, Dan tells me that if all we do is replace newspapers with sites like *The Huffington Post, Drudge Report,* or *Gawker,* "we have missed the point of what citizen media can be about, which is wider, deeper information, more useful to more people." He would like to see more citizen journalists, especially through nonprofit models, providing content that helps people find out what matters (gives them something to talk about).

The content citizen journalists produce may be outside mainstream media, but it can definitely affect personal, professional, and corporate reputations. So, Dan says, "smart companies will not be afraid of citizen media, but will learn from it and participate in the conversations."

## Something to Talk About in the Kitchen

Meet Thunder Parley, a Google software engineer and citizen journalist who bites the hand that feeds him every day. He's known throughout the Googleplex for his internal reviews of the company's 17 in-house cafés, where the food is free. Parley has no formal culinary training, but he does have plenty of opinions and he doesn't mind sharing them with anyone in the Google community who subscribes to his internal e-mail list.

Parley's opinions definitely make a difference. Once he sent out such a favorable review of the "Google bar" dessert that it caused a run on the cafés and 600 bars were gone in 30 minutes. Not surprisingly, his personal favorites tend to show up on Google's menus fairly regularly. No wonder Google's chefs compete—in a fun way—for high marks from Parley. Google's Pure Ingredient Café even cooked up a special hot sauce to suit Parley's taste for fiery condiments. "You're kind of blessed if you have Thunder in your building," says the executive chef.[4]

Think about how Parley affects Google's reputation inside and outside the organization. Free gourmet food is one of the company's legendary employee perks, part of the package Google uses to attract and keep the best and the brightest. In fact, it's one of the "Top 10 Reasons to Work at Google," according to the company's web site. You've probably read about the free food in Google's listing at the top of annual *Fortune's* "100 Best Companies to Work For" rankings. It's a very high profile aspect of working life at Google. So high profile, in fact, that Thunder Parley and his critiques have been the focus of articles in the *Los Angeles Times* and *Food Management* magazine, which is how I first heard about him.

Put yourself in the shoes of Google's management. You don't pay Parley to review your cafés (which he does on his lunch hour), but he is keeping your chefs on their toes. More important, he's helping to polish Google's reputation as a good employer. That has to be a positive for your employees and your ability to recruit new hires. Not only is citizen journalism contributing to Google's reputation, it's making Parley's personal reputation, as well.

## Advertising and Your Digital Rep

Companies can't control citizen journalists, but they can and do control their advertising. In World 2.0, what is the role of advertising in shaping the opinions and reputations of companies and products? It's clear that the days of the one-way ad are fading fast, the idea that if you just get in people's faces often enough they'll buy your product. Where does advertising go in a media world that is increasingly social? I can't believe the future is the 30- or 15-second intrusive TV commercial.

I talked with Paul LaVoie who, with Jane Hope, founded the Taxi ad agency in Toronto in 1992. Now the chairman of Taxi's six offices and based in NYC, Paul notes that reputation is important in creating "the kind of relationships you have with just about everyone—your employees, your vendors, and your clients. Reputation is established through behavior and that has been very important for Jane and me, because the reputation of our agency is based on how we create, who we hire, and the kind of work we do."

Paul believes the way brands work is consistent with what the leaders of the company decide are the values or beliefs the organization embodies. Executives make decisions and over time the way the company behaves signals what its reputation should be: advanced research . . . low price . . . high quality . . . quick sale . . . great design . . . in an infinite variety of combinations and permutations. "When I first started working in advertising," says Paul, "it was a monologue. People would see TV commercials or billboards, and they would form a perception." Today, he continues, "mass advertising can still be a very successful way to communicate and sell products and services, especially if you need to talk to a mass audience—but it can't stop there."

Advertising in World 2.0 needs to be more of a dialogue, because consumers now have the ability to go online and check out any advertising claim. Suppose a food company advertises its product as "the best Canola oil in the world." Its customers can check that claim by looking for blogs that compare Canola oils and sites where people discuss their experiences with the company and its products. Transparency and trust will have a lot to do with how consumers view that brand of Canola oil, which in turn will affect the company's reputation.

Knowing that consumers will go looking for information actually creates "an all-you-can-eat buffet of media opportunities for having conversations," Paul tells me. "Our mission is to create a spark, to start dialogues between consumers and companies." And in the fractured media landscape of World 2.0, small brands can get a conversation going just as easily as large brands. No wonder Paul says: "I really think that even more than the 1960s, the golden age of advertising creativity is right now."

The fractured media landscape may also mean that a small brand, product, or company with a superior product or service has an opportunity to build a reputation in ways it never had before. As Tony Perkins at AlwaysOn points out, Google was the fourteenth search engine to be established, but it had the best service: "It also had a cool name and a clean approach, but even without it, it had the best search and that was part of the black art of what Google did." Google quickly built a reputation, maintained its quality, and added features that continued to improve its reputation. Tony reminds me that excitement is not the same as reputation. You have to give your stakeholders something to talk about, but you also "have to deliver something of value or you won't be successful."

## There's a Moral to This Story

Last but not least, I want to talk for a moment about moral purpose, because this is a key element in reputation equity. (I'll discuss moral purpose in more detail in Chapter 9.) Whether you want to help end hunger or save the environment, incorporate this moral purpose into your online activities and invite customers, suppliers, and dealers to join you in this cause. When you click on the McDonald's U.S. home page, you can't miss the link to Ronald McDonald House Charities. When you walk into a McDonald's restaurant, you can't miss a poster or brochure about the charities. You know this is part of what McDonald's believes in.

Use your online destination to post your sustainability report, your report on the organization's progress toward integrated economic growth, environmental stewardship, and social responsibility. For example, British Petroleum has worked hard to establish itself as an environmentally responsible oil company. To avoid accusations of "greenwash," BP uses a sustainability reporting process based on internationally accepted guidelines issued by the Global Reporting Initiative. These are designed to ensure a company's environmental performance claims have a solid factual basis.

With its published report, BP publicizes its own "carbon footprint" and mounts advertising campaigns that promote consumer awareness of its energy conservation efforts and the availability of alternatives to oil and gas. The company's online Energy Calculator has attracted millions of visitors worldwide, helping to build BP's reputation as a credible leader in carbon and climate change discussions.[5]

Planning your online content also means planning where you want to be on the Web, as I'll discuss in the next chapter.

# Building Reputation: Where to Be on the Web

Ever wonder how you—or a friend—would look in Heidi Klum's or Beyonce's hairdo? *In Style* has the answer. The monthly magazine and its web site cover the latest fashion trends, celebrity looks, and beauty tips. *In Style* is also in on the current craze for widgets, bits of software that bring your content to your audience's desktop or blog or Facebook page *at their request*.

If you're not in the fashion magazine business, offering virtual makeovers may sound like a funny way to build a reputation. But *In Style* knows how much its readers care about the latest celebrity hair styles. That's why its web site includes a branded "Hollywood Hair Makeover" feature (http://www.instyle.com/instyle/makeover/). Readers simply upload their photos and try any of 100 celebrity hair styles, with new styles added every month. For this audience, the content is unique, relevant, and engaging.

Last year, the *In Style* site decided to take its online distribution a step further. It hired Buddy Media to create a widget that allows users to share makeover photos on their Facebook pages. In the first ten months, 300,000-plus people installed the widget and spent an average of seven minutes trying on different hairdos. Many of these people returned for virtual makeovers more than 25 times after installing the widget.[1]

The result: A branded experience that goes on and on, getting *In Style's* content to fashion fans around the Web and enhancing its reputation with every click. We'll talk more about widgets later, but they're only one of the many tools in your tool kit for getting your online content out on the Web where it can do the most good for your reputation.

## Your Place or Mine?

You've got your engagement strategy and your content. Now what? Don't just blow your content out on the Web; where, specifically, should you distribute it? Most organizations have many communities with which they need to work to build and manage reputation equity: customers, prospective customers, employees, vendors, stockholders, and regulators. Sometimes you need your own place (or places), the way Nike sponsors Nike+ as well as a host of other sites, and sometimes you can do just as well by dropping into other places on the Web.

E-communities are sites where people aggregate around a common interest and they often include professional content. People join these communities and return to them regularly because they offer news, information or advice, entertainment, or all three. You can connect with somebody else's e-community or build your own to reach the people who matter to your business.

Thousands of e-communities already draw sizable audiences, with new sites being established daily. The pioneer—and prototypical— e-community was Slate, which Microsoft founded in 1996. It's now owned by *The Washington Post* and has evolved into the Slate Group, an online publishing unit with several specialized news and opinion sites for targeted audiences.

By my definition, the main Slate site has a number of e-communities: news and politics, arts and life, business and technology, health and science, style and shopping, travel and food, and sports. These are communities not only because of the common interests members share, but because Slate's visitors can comment on and discuss the articles posted by the professional writers and reporters. Similarly, the AlwaysOn site I talked about in Chapter 4 has e-communities: GoingGreen, OnMedia, OnHollywood, and VC&$.

Lately I've noticed a lot of e-community activity around the topic of parenting, including sites like Babble, BabyCenter (owned by Johnson & Johnson), CafeMom (with advertisers such as General Mills, Wal-Mart, Target, P&G, Disney, and Unilever), UrbanBaby (part of the CNET Networks), and MothersClick (which includes user-contributed product reviews). Sites with broader content, such as iVillage, also have pages devoted to conversations among parents. What all this means is that if you want to build a reputation among parents, you have an opportunity to go to somebody else's party, mingle with the visitors, and maybe invite them to a party of your own.

For example, Kimberly-Clark's Huggies, which has established its own branded e-communities, like huggiesbabynetwork.com, also tried a pilot program by sponsoring 100 local Meetup parenting groups. Meetup.com is a social networking site, not an e-community; it hosts local groups that coordinate get-togethers among participants.

"We started with feedback from Meetup members and organizers as to whether they would want a sponsor and what they would find of value from a sponsor," says Brad Santeler, Kimberly-Clark's director for media and relationship marketing. "It's very transparent. We asked them what they wanted, and we're providing that." No stealth marketing here—everybody knows about the sponsorship angle. And it has real value to participants, because the company pays the monthly fees that these groups would ordinarily pay to Meetup. According to Kate Johnson, the company's consumer relationship marketing manager, "When you have one mom talking to another, it's powerful. So we're offering them information and tools and activities; we're not in their face with advertising."[2]

You can also tarnish your reputation with one poorly conceived effort at your own party, which is what happened to Motrin. Not long ago, McNeil Consumer Healthcare posted a commercial on its motrin .com site featuring a young mother saying: "Wearing your baby seems to be in fashion. I mean, in theory it's a great idea. There's the front baby carrier, sling, schwing, wrap, pouch. And who knows what else they've come up with. Wear your baby on your side, your front, go hands free. Supposedly, it's a real bonding experience. They say that babies carried close to the body tend to cry less than others. But what about me? Do moms that wear their babies cry more than those who don't? I sure do! These things put a ton of strain on your back, your neck, your shoulders. Did I mention your back? I mean, I'll put up with the pain because it's a good kind of pain; it's for my kid. Plus, it totally makes me look like an official mom. And so if I look tired and crazy, people will understand why."

As Lisa Belkin reported in her *New York Times* blog, "Online Moms did not respond to the ad by racing out for Motrin. They were offended by the suggestion that they carry their babies to be 'fashionable.' They were outraged at the idea that they look 'crazy.' They vehemently disagreed with the phrasing that 'in theory' carrying your baby around is a good idea."

Within hours of being posted, the ad was the most tweeted subject on Twitter. A day later, there was a nine-minute video on YouTube showing screen shots of the outraged twitter posts interspersed with photos of Moms carrying babies in slings. (It's still there: "Motrin Ad Makes Moms Mad" at http://www.youtube.com/watch?v=LhR-y1N6 R8Q&feature=related). Belkin says "a few bloggers and tweeters had gotten the ad agency that created the ad on the phone, to find they didn't know a lot about Twitter and didn't seem to have a clue that there was so much anger piling up online."

There was so much anger that Motrin immediately took the ad off its web site and Kathy Widmer, VP of marketing at McNeil, the person responsible for the brand, wrote to bloggers who'd been attacking the ad: "We certainly did not mean to offend moms through our advertising. Instead, we had intended to demonstrate genuine sympathy and appreciation for all that parents do for their babies. We believe deeply that moms know best and we sincerely apologize for disappointing you. Please know that we take your feedback seriously and will take swift action with regard to this ad. We are in the process of removing it from our web site. . . . "[3] But of course the damage had been done. I'll talk more about responding to negative comments in Chapter 11.

# What's In It for You?

E-communities can be excellent places for your company to participate in the discussions. It's important to distinguish e-communities from, say, social networking communities such Facebook, MySpace, YouTube, or Meetup for that matter. Some e-communities contain largely professional content with a leaven of reader comment, while others mix user-generated with some professional content.

When you want to build your reputation by connecting with your most valued stakeholders at the online places where they gather, think about the opportunities that e-communities can open up. Car enthusiasts flock to motortrend.com, caranddriver.com, edmunds.com, and similar sites to get the latest automotive news, read blogs, exchange opinions about concept cars, and so on. If you want to build your reputation in the automotive field, you should be involved with popular car sites. If you're an airline, a resort, or a cruise ship company, you should be involved with travel sites such as TripAdvisor, Lonely Planet, Dopplr, and Slow Travel.

E-communities allow participants to get involved with other people who share their interests, whether it's cars or travel. It is almost as easy for the automotive supplier or the hotel company to engage their stakeholders. If I were in the pharmaceutical/life sciences industries, I'd want to ensure a presence in the most topical e-communities that draw sizable audiences, such as WebMD's different communities.

Because of your monitoring, you should know where your stakeholders gather online and what issues they care about. Be visible and active in e-communities where those key issues are discussed; be transparent about who you are and who you represent. Be sure your content adds to the discussion rather than blatantly plugging your brand. Building trust will build your reputation.

If you're Genzyme and you know your stakeholders are regularly logging onto WebMD, try sharing information in the chat areas, or on the bulletin boards, or posting questions for visitors to answer. Or participate in the e-community's blog to raise awareness of your company and what it's doing. If somebody is commenting on a site, you can comment as well (and comment on the comments). The thread keeps going, and, on the Web, it exists forever. Make yourself part of the e-community conversation.

I believe e-communities will become the preferred resource for today's generation, the way magazines were for an older generation. The parents of yesterday had *Parents*, the parents of today have Babble.com as well as the print and e-community versions of *Parents*. The older generation had *Forbes*, the new generation has Forbes .com. The big difference is that in the older world, magazines, newspapers, radio, and television were one-way communication. In the e-communities, members take only what they want, take as much as they want, and talk back.

## Here, There, Nearly Everywhere

It's hard to exaggerate the number of ways you can engage your audience through creative distribution of content. Everyone needs to be thinking about making all content portable and using all the different platforms at your disposal. It's all about time and place shifting and, eventually, destination shifting. In other words, you want visitors to be able to view your content on your destination site and also be able to embed it into their MySpace or Facebook profiles, on their blogs, in their web sites, or download it to their cell phones. Mobile channels and endpoints such as the iPhone will eventually eclipse the computer base, so think ahead about future destinations.

If you want to build a reputation in a proactive way, the cell phone is becoming more and more important. With 3G it becomes simpler to digest web-based content, especially on the iPhone. (3G, based on International Telecommunication Union standards, is the third generation of standards and technology for mobile networking. 3G networks, which have yet to become commonplace in the United States, offer more advanced services than earlier networks: wide-area wireless voice telephony, video calls, and broadband wireless data.) Global giants such as Samsung, Sony Ericsson, and Nokia already have 3G phones on the market in other countries and more manufacturers are readying their own models.

These new networks and devices will make it easier for consumers on the go to visit you on the Web for audio content, text content, video content, or all three. Already there are more mobile phones that are able to pluck data from the Web than there are computers, a gap that will only grow larger. This trend is so important that Google recently tweaked its mobile format so the results better fit the screen and load more quickly on iPhones (and on phones using its Google Android software).

Here's how Audi is building its reputation for cutting-edge technology by connecting with car enthusiasts who access the Web by computer and mobile phone. When the company set up a site for its Q5 auto, not yet available in the United States, it offered the usual photos and specs plus free Q5 photos on "wallpaper" for visitors to download and use to decorate their virtual desktops. Then it added the Audi MobileCam, a mobile application that enabled visitors to digitally add a Q5 to their own photos and click to send the results to their friends. The final photo might show a couple standing against a Q5 in their own driveway or a driver behind the wheel of a Q5 cruising underwater or up the side of a skyscraper. Recipients could view the forwarded photo on their cell phones and click to join the fun by visiting the Q5 site themselves. In the first week alone, more than 1,500 people downloaded the Audi MobileCam.[4]

Considering that the Q5 wouldn't hit the showrooms for months, this was a good way for Audi to get its content to an interested audience. It also polished Audi's reputation by showing how well the automaker knows its audience—that they're big users of cell phones and they like to interact with technology. Yes, the product played a big role, but the beauty of this mobile app was that it let car enthusiasts be the stars of their own show. And it sparked lots of conversations between Audi and car enthusiasts as well as between car fans and their friends.

## To Cast a Wide Net

If you want to build your reputation across a mass audience, consider putting a video (or two or three) on YouTube. Although Chapter 10 is entirely devoted to the YouTube juggernaut, I want to mention it here because of its powerful reach. This is your chance to tell your story exactly as you want it told. If your video is featured on the YouTube home page, your views go straight out. It might not be the qualified audience that you're looking to achieve, but you will get a broad cross-section of the U.S. population and, increasingly, more viewers in Europe.

To attract an audience, your video must have value for the viewer and be engaging without being manipulative. If people don't watch, then your video won't go up in the rankings—and if it doesn't go up in the rankings, it won't be highlighted on YouTube's home page and you won't get much traction there.

With a little luck and a lot of views, your video could go viral and add to your reputation on a large scale. When you cast a wide net using video, you have to understand the nitty-gritty of distributing through different sites. One site might sample the first ten seconds of your video; another might display the middle frame from your video.

Once your content is out on the Web, it may appear in different ways on different sites and different devices. Keep this in mind for text you add to your web site, blog, or Twitter. If you have something relevant to say, others will link to it or cut and paste it into their own posts (or both), gaining you wider distribution. But you can't know in advance who's going to join the conversation or when.

## Making Widgets Work

Do you have a widget strategy? Wikipedia describes a web widget as "a portable chunk of code that can be installed and executed within any separate HTML-based web page by an end user without requiring additional compilation. They are derived from the idea of code reuse. Other terms used to describe web widgets include: gadget, badge, module, webjit, capsule, snippet, mini and flake . . . Widgets often take the form of on-screen tools (clocks, event countdowns, auction-tickers, stock market tickers, flight arrival information, daily weather, etc)."

The most effective widgets are so useful that they encourage ongoing interaction between you and your audience. *Ad Age's*

Bob Garfield is a big fan of widgets, which he calls a "magical con-nection between marketers and consumers, not only replacing the one-way messaging long dominated by media advertising but vastly outperforming it. Because online, the link is literal and direct, and along its path, data of behavior, preference and intention are left at every step."

Garfield observes that target audiences search for a desirable widget, keep it on their virtual desktop or install it in their web browser, and pass copies to friends. Best of all, he says, "the barriers to entry are preposterously low." Garfield singles out the virtual desktop widget "Miles," which coordinates with Nike+ (see previous chapter) to help you track your running progress, find out about running events, and even organize RSS feeds to download to your iPod.[5]

What about distributing widgets through bloggers? Bloggers are always looking for new content and interesting things to engage their audiences. A widget is not going to cannibalize their traffic, because people are already visiting their sites and digesting the content. Of course, the widget won't appeal to bloggers or enhance your reputa-tion unless it has value to the people who visit these blogs.

Here's an example from Digital Influence Group's work for T-Mobile. The company wanted to promote a cost-effective, reliable telephone service for the home. It's not a cell phone nor does it require a landline because it uses the Internet; it offers the mobility of a cell without the cost. T-Mobile identified mothers as being one of the markets for the technology, and wanted to generate awareness of this device among mothers.

DIG, where I am chairman, reached out to bloggers who write for mothers and found 10 who would host a T-Mobile contest. DIG built a widget, an interactive box that had the look and feel of each indi-vidual mommy blogger site. It looked like something else you would find on that destination. The box had a question relevant to moth-ers and the blog. These were questions like: "What features from your mobile phone would you like on your home phone?" "Do you have a home phone; why or why not?" "Who do you talk to the most on your phone?" "What age do you think is appropriate for your child to be allowed to answer the phone?" The box included the T-Mobile logo and an invitation to enter a contest to win a home by clicking through.

Visitors who answered the question were eligible for the random drawings with daily, weekly, and grand prizes. DIG went through the results and randomly chose winners for the smaller prizes. Women who clicked through learned more about T-Mobile and the new service. At the end of the two-week contest, visitors to the 10 blogs had submitted 3,187 comments. There were 562 total clicks on the banners within the widget, leading to the "Ultimate Home Giveaway" microsite and 46,338 total impressions. In the end, the bloggers, the visitors, and T-Mobile were all happy.

The bloggers were happy because the widget brought comments and traffic to their blogs. They liked that the widget, although clearly identified with T-Mobile, was not intrusive. Nonparticipating bloggers linked to, or posted about, the contest building further awareness and some told DIG that they were available and interested in participating in future contests.

Visitors left comments like "Thanks so much for this giveaway. Wouldn't it be great to have many of the same features on your home phone as on your cell? Never thought of this before, but now I love this idea." "Great prize, I would love to learn to work all the gadgets that come with the new phones. Thanks for the contest." "What a super contest. We would LOVE a home! I'm so impressed that they joined with you too. I'd love to know how to start getting sponsors for contests like you do. . . . "

T-Mobile was pleased not only because the effort raised awareness among key prospects for their product, but because they now have a widget that the firm can use in the future. Change the target, change the questions, change the widget's look and they're good to go. They also have some rough measures of features people would like to see on their home phones.

The contest helped build T-Mobile's reputation with this market because it was all about the destination and working with that specific audience; by design the content was not intrusive. It was designed to stimulate a conversation among mothers and the mommy blogger.

We were starting the conversation. There was no right answer to the questions. If a visitor wanted the commercial, we gave them the ability to watch it but we did not push it.

This is the way to build your digital reputation: If you are entering someone's world, you have to talk their talk. Social media fosters conversation. The proof of the success is the number of comments you are getting as people respond to these widgets. Many people answered these simple T-Mobile questions because they were simple, because they were relevant, and because they were directed to their interests. The answers, by the way, were available to anybody who went to the blog; nothing was hidden.

For me, the success of social media comes down to conversation. The trick is to have a conversation in a way that helps your reputation. Start by knowing your audience; what are they looking for? It's the same as going to a cocktail party. You verbally give . . . you take . . . you learn . . . you listen. You don't walk in with a megaphone and start shouting.

## New Places to Be on the Web

No matter where you distribute your content today, keep your eyes peeled for the next hot new destination. Tomorrow you might have to be on FriendFeed (http://friendfeed.com) or Jaiku (http://jaiku.com). FriendFeed keeps you up-to-date on the web pages, photos, videos, and music your friends and family are sharing. You can customize a feed of the content your friends shared—from news articles to family photos to interesting links and videos. FriendFeed automatically imports shared stuff from sites across the Web—including your company's content, if users choose it.

Jaiku, now a part of Google, allows people to share their activity streams, essentially a log of everyday things as they happen. You can share your messages, recommendations, events as they happen, or photos as soon as you snap them. Content can be posted directly to Jaiku or added using web feeds. Jaiku Mobile is a live phonebook that displays the activity streams, availability, and location of your Jaiku contacts. This is another place where content might be shared to gain a wider audience.

There are two pitfalls to consider when planning your distribution strategy. First, move now to register domains and names on sites that matter to you and your audiences. *Business Week* reports that a British site called Twitter Names Parked has registered and is selling names such as INGDirect, StephenKing, and FordMotor. Even if you're not going to use any of these names now, you want the flexibility to do so later.

Second, be on the lookout for imposters. After Exxon Mobil learned that someone who called herself "Janet" was posing as an employee when sending tweets, the company talked with Twitter, which shut her account down. "Twitter doesn't allow impersonation or domain squatting, which is grabbing a user name and saying you want money," explains Twitter's Biz Stone.[6]

The principle here is the same as in marketing a product or service; you want to be where your target market is. The difference in building your reputation is that you're not trying to sell something; you're trying to be a good corporate citizen. This may mean simply participating in conversations about issues that affect your industry. It may mean establishing a web site like Chevron's willyoujoinus where people who care about an issue can express themselves, read other people's opinions, and draw their own conclusions. If they're going to talk about you anyway, you should consider providing the forum and setting the tone.

Last year, when American car makers were appealing to Congress for money, General Motor's vice chairman Robert Lutz wrote on the corporation's FastLane blog: "It's been a historic week for us, and I don't mean in Washington. And let me just say upfront that I know there is a lot of talk online about that subject. But I am not going to comment here about any government loans or hearings or GM's financial situation—just like I wouldn't engage you in conversation about it if I ran into you in the produce aisle." Rather, he said, he wanted to talk about the Chevrolet Volt, GM's electric car.

When I visited the blog, I noticed a few public comments questioning why Lutz wouldn't post messages about the loans. "Why not?" asked one. " . . . I think it would be good for you to talk with ordinary people about GM's situation. You need to hear viewpoints other than what you get discussing it in the executive suites at the Ren Cen or over cocktails at the Bloomfeld Hills C.C."

However, the majority of the comments were supportive, technical, advice-filled, or all three. "Lutz is known and respected in auto circles everywhere," wrote Julia Hood, the publishing director of *PR Week*. "His genuine zeal for cars gives him the kind of authenticity that resonates with analysts, media members, and enthusiasts alike."[7] General Motors encouraging a senior executive to express his unbuttoned opinions can only help its reputation.

As I've said before, your content will be online for a long time, possibly forever, thanks to Internet archive sites. Even those Audi photos I mentioned earlier could live on in cell-phone memories for quite a while. That's why you need to think ahead about destinations as well as content. With good planning, your audiences will be able to see, interact with, and share the most reputation-enhancing material on their own sites and screens now and in the future. This requires a host of new roles and new jobs, which I'll discuss in the next chapter.

# This Means New Roles, New Jobs for Every Organization

In the last four chapters, I've talked about monitoring the Web, starting dialogues, finding something to talk about, and deciding where to be. Sounds great, but who's going to do it? Somebody has to be in charge whether the organization is a small business or a multibillion dollar corporation.

Someone has to watch the landscape, not just social media, but all media. What is the tone? Where are the discussions happening? How important are the comments? The challenge today is that the discussions may affect many parts of the company—finance, human resources, manufacturing, shipping, legal, government affairs, as well as sales, marketing, and customer relations.

This means that no department is an island (or a silo). The days when the customer relations department could be off by itself answering consumer letters and phone calls are gone. The days when the public relations department counted clippings to report how many times the company was mentioned positively or negatively and whether the message was getting through are long gone. Today there is no line between customer relations/public relations and reputation.

## Digital Facilitator

The overall role I'm describing is that of digital facilitator, someone whose role is to continue constructive conversations around the topics, products, and issues the company wants to talk about. If you're an oil company, you want conversations about energy policy. If you're a pharmaceutical company, you want conversations about health care. Somebody has to have the responsibility, the time, the information, the authority, and the resources to monitor discussions and post timely comments—that's the digital facilitator.

The digital facilitator has the company's best interests at heart, yet he or she must also be transparent in all dialogues. For example, I have a friend who is head of investor relations for a major corporation. His firm was often in the news as the sub-prime credit crisis grew. The issues here are incredibly complex; few reporters understand the subtleties and even fewer have the space and time to explain the issues clearly. As a result, many of the news reports, blogs, and comments were, to be kind, one-sided and inaccurate. Inadvertently— or not—reporters were dragging the corporation's reputation through the mud.

My friend always monitors online and offline media for mentions of his company. Whenever he found inaccurate comments, he immediately wrote clear, careful, truthful, and accurate responses and e-mailed these to influential securities analysts, fund managers, and other key individuals. Notice that he made his case directly to the investment community rather than to the media outlets or the bloggers. Because his recipients trust him—he has built a positive reputation over the years—they trust his analysis and he has been able to minimize the damage to his company's reputation and stock price.

## Beyond Webmaster

You know what a webmaster is (and presumably your company has one or more). In World 2.0, your company will require new roles and new jobs to achieve what Ted Smyth, chief administrative officer and senior vice president, corporate & government affairs of H.J. Heinz, calls "mastery of digital media to foster a real dialogue with audiences."[1] In other words, to build and protect your digital reputation.

What exactly are these new jobs? Here's a sampling of job titles: Fodors.com has a community manager; Hewlett-Packard has an editor-in-chief for web site content; Dell has a VP of communities and conversations to oversee, well, e-communities and online conversations (he blogs and tweets as well); Intercontinental Hotels Group has a social marketing manager who also examines the ROI of the firm's social marketing; Graco has a social media manager who doubles as blog guide for the baby product company; Nokia has a blogger outreach team (to engage influential bloggers) and editors for its Nokia Conversations blogs.

These job titles don't even cover all the new roles that managers and employees will play in World 2.0. I see three categories of roles and jobs: (1) editors (for content and dialogue), (2) distribution, and (3) publisher (the manager who's ultimately responsible for the company's overall digital rep strategy, implementation, and evaluation). In a small business, the owner/manager may have to wear all these hats. The larger the company, the more complex the jobs and the more people will be involved in these roles.

And remember, your company will probably not have new funding for these new roles and jobs, especially in the current economic climate. Which is why Pauline Ores, principal analyst, social media engagement at IBM, points out two challenges in clarifying and assigning new roles: "These are resource-intensive programs that require sizable investment and long-term commitment. In addition to articulating business value, you have to outline activities this will replace or supplement—in essence, develop a broader business model outlining the benefits of shifting resources from here to there. Similarly, delivering optimum business value requires integrating new and existing roles, activities, and systems—an overall transformation of what you have in place today, which will be measured in months, if not years, and certainly not weeks." Pauline is deep into the issues of new roles and new jobs because she works on social-networking strategies for IBM, assesses where social media and search marketing can add value, and determines how to integrate social media marketing into the company's existing programs—all critical to managing digital rep.

Despite the challenge of limited budgets, and despite our current economic reality, building a digital reputation must be a high priority in World 2.0. This is a given—so what new jobs and roles must your organization have in place to do this?

## Monitors for World 2.0

As I discussed in Chapter 2, you need to know who's talking about you and what they're saying, online and offline. That's why you need one or more employees to set up and follow search alerts and use other tools for monitoring the content, tone, and volume of online conversations that concern you and your industry. Your monitors must be diving into the digital universe at all times to keep the organization informed about what's going on.

Monitors should know how much weight to put on the comments of one blogger versus another or the participants in one forum versus another. They should also note the kinds of questions customers are asking each other, the kinds of complaints customers are posting, the way stakeholders talk about competitors and the industry, and the pertinent issues raised by regulators.

Content monitors should be especially attuned to early warning signs of online rumors. If they're not authorized to respond to comments, questions, or rumors, they should be able to arrange for a speedy response from elsewhere in the organization and summarize what's happening for management attention.

In some organizations, content monitors may play a role in analyzing the firm's reputation at different points in time and interpreting changes in the direction and the strength of trends based on key attributes. For instance, the home page of St. Jude Children's Hospital includes a link titled "Your Opinion Matters," which leads to a quick survey aimed at potential and current donors. Just a few screens long, it closes with a request to e-mail the hospital's market research people with additional thoughts, questions, or concerns. Someone has to monitor the results of these surveys and follow up. In other organizations, actual reputation monitoring may be the realm of researchers on staff or an outside research agency.

## Editors Provide Something to Talk About

Another key role is that of editor, which is not the same as a newspaper or video editor. In World 2.0, editors may or may not actually develop and script the content, but they're responsible for the material (both verbal and visual) you present online. For instance, you may have one editor planning content for your YouTube videos and a different editor planning material for web site pages or blogs. I want to mention some specific roles that fall into this category:

- *Blogger.* Your blogger or bloggers may be solely responsible for blogging or may have other duties as well; they may be deep in the organization (possibly technical experts), or in public relations or marketing, or even at the top of the hierarchy. Your bloggers may not even be sitting at their keyboards when they blog. Marriott International's CEO, Bill Marriott, voice-records his blog entries for staff to transcribe and post in his name. His blog (http://www .blogs.marriott.com) includes the audio version, which adds a human touch. The blog reaches external and internal audiences (about 20 percent of the 6,000 weekly visitors are hotel employees). And who thought up the idea of Marriott's CEO blog? The company's head of global communications, as one of her new roles.

Here's an excerpt from Marriott's first blog entry in January, 2007: "I'm venturing into uncharted territory as I launch this blog. A year ago, I didn't even know what a blog was—until my Communications team began telling me about all the blog traffic on travel and tourism. Now I know this is where the action is if you want to talk to your customers directly—and hear back from them."[2]

Sometimes the blogging role comes under the marketing umbrella. Randy Tinseth, vice president of marketing for Boeing Commercial Airplanes, fills the role of that company's official blogger by writing

Randy's Journal (http://boeingblogs.com/randy/). By coincidence, Boeing's previous official blogger was Randy Baseler, who was vice president of marketing before Randy Tinseth.

In addition, you may have one or more people microblogging on Twitter, which as I've already noted requires extreme brevity and a steady stream of new tweets. Dell employees tweet about the company; Dell has offers and provides news updates on Twitter. If you want to engage stakeholders via Twitter, you'll need to determine who will fulfill this content role at your organization.

One more point: Your bloggers ought to know how to tag entries appropriately (so stakeholders can find entries and join the conversation) and how to add links to enrich the content (so stakeholders can dig deeper and find out more about the topic). As small as these details seem to be, they make a big difference in your ability to keep up a running dialogue with stakeholders.

- *Social networking editor.* If you have a company or brand page on Facebook and other social network sites, you'll need to be sure someone in your organization keeps them current, reads and responds to comments and questions, and adds new content and connections. This is an interactive role, which may include participating in social media discussions on your pages/sites and getting involved in discussions on other relevant social networking sites.

- *E-community moderator.* E-community moderator (or e-community manager) is a must role for companies that establish their own e-communities to engage stakeholders. Here's an excerpt from a job description for Community Manager posted by the blogtech firm Apture, which describes the ideal candidate as having: "an infectious passion for making the web a better, richer, more engaging place; a track record of growing and managing online communities; you enjoy hands-on contact with the community and directly helping them solve their problems; you are a web and community evangelist that can direct the community culture and be the outward voice of the company." Your e-community moderator may welcome first-time posters, keep conversations going, and weed out inappropriate comments.

- *Responders*. Who in your company has the authority to respond when monitoring turns up the need? This is a vital role that has a direct bearing on your digital rep. Elliot Schrage, vice president of communications at Facebook, says that in a 24-hour news cycle (and that's what we're now living in), organizations no longer have the ability to make communications or public relations decisions in the traditional hierarchical fashion. "You don't have time to get the CEO or even the chief communications officer to sign off, because the crisis may be happening or the issue may be surfacing when everybody is asleep," he tells me. "And you can't wait for six or eight hours, when everybody gets up, to respond."

Moreover, the CEO, CFO, or CMO may not be particularly sensitive to the circumstances, the local culture, or the relevance of every issue. It's often more effective (and certainly faster) to delegate to someone who's closer to the customer. Remember the Comcast example I cited in Chapter 2, where an executive who was monitoring Twitter and blogs called an unhappy customer who had tweeted about his experience? That exec also arranged for a tech team to resolve the customer's problem. So you may wind up with responders who speak for the company and responders who follow up to address the immediate situation.

- *Privacy and legal issues*. Who in your organization will devise your privacy policy and be sure your opt-in and opt-out procedures follow the law? Who will let your company's bloggers know what's off limits and help responders deal with problem posters or rumors with legal implications? Who will monitor the blogosphere and social networking sites for copyright infringement (and take steps to correct the problem)?

## Dealing with Distribution

Distribution involves being in the right places at the right times. The person or people responsible will have to know where the organization ought to be represented. What web sites are the most important for their reviews of the company's products or services? What bloggers have the most influence among the company's stakeholders? What stakeholders—employees, customers, vendors, analysts—have the greatest impact on the company's reputation?

Let me mention some specific roles that deal with distribution, with the caveat that these roles may overlap and should, in fact, not be stand-alone or silos but should involve broad internal communication and contact:

- *Media Distribution.* Who's in charge of ensuring that your online presence aimed at reporters, bloggers, and other members of the media is up-to-date, complete, ready, and responsive? You'll need more than the basic background facts. For instance, IBM's online press room (at www-03.ibm.com/press/us/en/index.wss) offers news releases with links embedded, which makes it easy for reporters to get more info with a couple of clicks, as well as video and animation in some releases. It also offers dozens of RSS news feeds; multimedia press kits geared to specific events or issues; photos and videos for journalists to download; and a link to a brief online feedback form ("Your feedback will help us improve this site. If you have comments or questions about the IBM Press Room site, please fill out this form and someone from IBM Communications will contact you shortly."). Asking for feedback is a nice touch, it shows that IBM is fostering dialogue rather than pushing its messages in one-way fashion.

- *Public Relations.* I'll have a lot more to say about this in Chapter 12, but for now here's a quote from Ted Smyth that summarizes the challenge and opportunity: "The PR professional of the future needs to transform PR from public relations to personal relations."[3] And another quote from my conversation with Idil Cakim, vice president of interactive media at Golin Harris: "Future PR executives will need to understand not only how to reach out to online media, and how to engage bloggers, but also understand online relationship management. The same way they understand TV, print, radio, and other traditional outlets, they will need to understand online dynamics and how to build and manage online communities and relationships."

- *Search Engine Optimization.* What do the first organic results pages indicate about your company's reputation? How can you use search engines to improve your visibility and reputation? "Amazingly enough, a lot of companies are still not doing as much as they should be doing with search," comments Pauline Ores at IBM. "You do see search engine optimization and paid search going up, even as marketing budgets are going down, because they are more cost-effective. In some ways, the weak economy forces people to take the time and make the effort to find something more efficient and to try something new because they have to." Who in your organization is looking at search engines?

- *Metrics.* "There are metrics that you can measure, such as how many people read a particular blog post and how many commented," Pauline tells me. "But you have to link that metric back to the business. What we really want to measure is the business value and that is the Holy Grail right now for most of us." The exact metrics will differ from company to company, of course, but the important thing here is to have someone assigned to handle metrics.

- *Widgets.* If you want to offer widgets, you'll need someone to handle that (or manage the agency you hire to create them). Widgets will soon be everywhere. Browsing the Heinz web site, I ran across its widget for Facebook and MySpace, which involves a ketchup "squeeze" (see http://www.heinz.com/widget.aspx), but can also be delivered via e-mail. Be sure your widgets people talk to your metrics people—you'll need to know how many people install your widgets, how viral they are, and so forth. If they're not achieving your objectives, you should know as soon as possible.

## Introducing the Publisher

The publisher is the responsible manager who oversees World 2.0 activities on behalf of the company, ensures consistency with overall corporate strategy, has a clear vision of how to build and sustain digital rep, and is ultimately responsible for content. The publisher understands and embraces the organization's moral purpose (more about that in Chapter 9) and sees the connection between moral purpose and reputation.

The publisher's role has changed as digital dialogues replace one-way communication in traditional media. Formerly, says Facebook's Elliot Schrage, "the communication function was a fairly tactical or operational function. How do we get the story out about X? How do we generally tell the story about the company? And who is particularly good at executing those? The communication function was really how do we most effectively communicate the message?"

Schrage observes that the digital world has brought new demands and requirements: "The organization is moving away from simply telling a narrative to using narratives to express its values. Reputation becomes the expression of a company's core values, because the rate of activity and the volume of information is so great that rather than focusing on specific story lines or narrative, reputation consists of the consistent expression of values." In other words, the publisher has to understand the underlying values and be sure they're consistently communicated through all online activities, dialogues, and media. This is a significant role that is difficult to capture in a simple job description.

Elliot also makes the point that "professionals need to be much more talented and much more strategically oriented at all levels of the communication organization than in the past. Rather than building hierarchical organizations, which is how organization teams have been built in the past, you need profoundly decentralized organizations that are moving along a consistent path to advance values, or for reputation. The hiring I do and the professional development I promote focuses on these issues that distinguish today's communications professional from yesterday's professional."

Because a large organization touches so many stakeholders, these new roles/new jobs must be dispersed throughout the organization. Management's task is coordination rather than maintaining a hierarchy. In effect, the publisher must be a superb coordinator, not a powerful commander-in-chief. Monitors, responders, and bloggers may sit in different departments, a challenge for the publisher but also an opportunity to bring many minds and viewpoints to the table to polish your digital rep.

In major corporations, the publisher might double as the chief engagement officer, ensuring that employees and managers are engaging when and where they should, all around the digital universe. Or this may be the responsibility of a different manager, who collaborates with the publisher to cover all the bases of values and engagement.

A smaller organization may have fewer people, but the principles and the functions remain the same. Someone must monitor what is being said on the Web, someone must respond and keep the conversations going, and someone must see that the organization has a presence where it does the most good. Your publisher may wear many hats, perhaps blogger-in-chief or some other role. A small business owner may be a monitor but not a responder, or a publisher but not a monitor or editor. The bottom line is that most of the roles I've described in this chapter must be covered in one way or another, but exactly how is up to every organization to decide.

In Chapter 7, I will talk about a topic that touches you personally—your personal digital rep.

# It's All About You (and Your Firm)

# Click—*Your* Personal Reputation at Stake

According to Reid Hoffman, the founder and CEO of LinkedIn, you don't have just one personal reputation— you have both a foreground reputation and a background reputation.

"Your foreground reputation comes from how you present yourself to other people," Reid tells me. In the digital world, your foreground reputation evolves from what you deliberately put out about yourself on the Web—the images and words you post, the sites and networks you join, the people and organizations you publicly align yourself with (or take a stand against). "You want your foreground reputation to say, 'Here's who I am' so people will see you as someone they want to do business with," Reid says.

Your background reputation comes from what people learn about you from other sources. In the real world, this is what one person says about you to another person. In the digital world, this is what is available to a diligent web surfer. "Background reputation is how people check you out with their own resources, not the information that you put out about yourself," Reid explains. Because your background reputation is not under your direct control, people who take the time to search out this information online find it particularly credible.

Together, your foreground and background reputations add up to your personal digital rep. And just what is your personal digital rep worth?

## The $50 Billion Power of Digital Rep

One of the most newsworthy examples of the power of digital rep comes directly from recent headlines. Potential clients and investment managers interested in Bernard L. Madoff Securities LLC could learn from searching the Web that the founder was a former chairman of Nasdaq, served on a government advisory panel for stock-market regulation, sat on several charitable boards, and started a family foundation. Moreover, as his supporters reported, Madoff's fund consistently returned 10 to 12 percent a year, regardless of market swings. That was Madoff's background rep.

Here's a taste of his foreground rep, as shaped by what was posted on the company's web site: "In an era of faceless organizations owned by other equally faceless organizations, Bernard L. Madoff Investment Securities LLC harks back to an earlier era in the financial world: The owner's name is on the door. Clients know that Bernard Madoff has a personal interest in maintaining the unblemished record of value, fair-dealing, and high ethical standards that has always been the firm's hallmark."[1]

As Madoff's personal reputation grew, so did his fund. Wall Street sophisticates and Hollywood tycoons entrusted their money to Madoff, as did nonprofit foundations, municipal pension funds, and the International Olympic Committee. "Adding to Mr. Madoff's allure was his exclusivity," *The Wall Street Journal* reported. "Investors had to be invited to join, and could be thrown off at will. When one client sent an e-mail to other clients that recounted a conversation with Mr. Madoff, an agent called and threatened to expel the investor from the fund, according to that investor."[2]

Despite Madoff's decades-long reputation for investment savvy and his close links to the financial community, his empire came crashing down after he pleaded guilty to running what amounted to a

Ponzi scheme. Madoff's reputation was not, it turns out, reality. The machinations cost investors worldwide an estimated $50 billion and sent tremors reverberating through the already shaky global economic situation. The legal, financial, and economic consequences will be felt for years.

What happened after Madoff's meltdown illustrates another important point I want to make: Your personal reputation can be tarnished by association, even if you have no direct connection with whoever is sinking your boat. Given the high profile of the Madoff case and the huge losses involved, it's not surprising that people might begin to question the reputations of other people in the investment field.

As James B. Stewart wrote in *The Wall Street Journal*, not long after the Madoff case made headlines: "I spoke last week to a money manager with an unblemished reputation who had just spent four hours defending herself to a client who said she couldn't trust anyone in the wake of the Madoff scandal." Stewart's conclusion: "Mr. Madoff is an especially shocking example, but he is an aberration. The vast majority of money managers are honest, hard-working professionals with their clients' best interests at heart."[3]

Just as a good reputation is essential in the investment world, it's vitally important to every seller on eBay. Two academics—Luis M. B. Cabral at NYU's Stern School of Business and Ali Hortacsu at the University of Chicago—have studied this issue in great detail. They constructed a panel of eBay seller histories and examined the importance of eBay's reputation mechanism. They found that when a seller first receives negative feedback, his or her weekly sales rate drops from a positive 7 percent to a negative 7 percent. Subsequent negative feedback ratings, however, have less impact than the initial negative ratings.

Cabral and Hortacsu found that the lower an eBay seller's reputation, the higher the likelihood that he or she would stop selling. In fact, just before exiting, sellers received more negative feedback than their lifetime average ratings.[4] Maybe you always suspected that sellers thrive or die on eBay based on their reputations, but now you know for sure.

## Put Yourself in the Foreground

Figure 7.1 outlines the steps to building your personal reputation in World 2.0. As I discussed in Chapter 2, you must monitor what people are saying online about you and your company—your background rep. Don't just search for your name (and variations) once or twice. Set up ongoing alerts for your name (including any professional variations, such as with and without middle initial) and have search results delivered to your e-mailbox at least weekly. While you're at it, set alerts to search for the names of people who matter to you, personally and professionally.

Next, identify and prioritize your personal/professional stakeholders. Who do you want to present yourself to and how do you want to

- Monitor personal/professional mentions of your name on blogs, web sites, tweets, social-networking pages, company sites, retail sites, and so on.
- Analyze positive and negative aspects of your current digital rep.
- Identify your personal/professional "stakeholders" (friends and colleagues, current and potential employers, current and potential customers, professional contacts, others).
- Set priorities for making a positive impression on these stakeholders and, if necessary, for improving your rep.
- Determine which e-communities and sites matter to your stakeholders and your firm, industry, and career.
- Establish a personal and/or professional home on the web (claim your name as a web domain, blog, etc.) and regularly update your content.
- Become active in personal/professional social-networking sites/systems.
- Be judicious in linking to others, recommending others, and having others recommend you.
- Select specific destinations for joining the online conversation and contribute (thoughtfully and respectfully) to discussion threads, blog posts, reviews, and so on.
- Keep commenting, blogging, or reviewing under the same name so you show up in search results.
- Continue monitoring your digital rep, tweak tactics as needed.

**Figure 7.1**  Managing *Your* Online Reputation

introduce yourself online? What dialogues do you want to spark? Now you're ready to begin laying the foundation on which your personal digital reputation—particularly your foreground reputation—will be built.

The first building block you'll need is a personal or professional web site, which is easy and free (or at least inexpensive) to set up. If you're a consultant, a lawyer, or an entrepreneur, meaning you and the business share a name and reputation, you may want to hire a web site designer to create something more original and elaborate than the off-the-shelf free web site templates offer.

What do you put on your web site? Whatever you'd like visitors—strangers, especially your stakeholders—to know about you: Your picture, your background, your accomplishments, your interests, your hobbies, plus links to your blog. Your goal here is to make a positive impression and present yourself as an authority in your field.

Another building block can be one or more sub-domains on your web site. For example, whitepapers.example.com and podcasts .example.com could be sub-domains of the example.com domain. Organizations use sub-domains to assign a unique name to a particular department, function, or service related to the organization. Individuals who want to showcase several aspects of their careers or personal interests might consider sub-domains like speeches, books, articles, podcasts, or videos. As you decide what to include on your site, think about what will most enhance your foreground reputation.

Your own blog and comments you post on other blogs are the next building blocks. Once people start to see your comments in other places, they're more likely to search for your personal or professional home on the Web. Even if you can't control what's said about you on other sites, your own blog, home page, and tweets are under *your* control. That's why blogging should be high on your list of activities to enhance your personal online reputation.

Chris Alden, chairman and CEO of the blog software and services company Six Apart, tells me: "Whatever the topic, whether it be economics, technology, politics, food, or entertainment, blogs have a major influence over ideas, trends, and analysis of the news of the day. To properly communicate online, you now need an identity with which to communicate, and the blog can be a big part of that.

Many people have an identity through their social networking profiles, but these are fairly cookie-cutter. The blog is a chance to expand that online identity and use it as a point to converse with other people online."

Although a blog is an excellent platform for expressing your views, Chris emphasizes that it doesn't have to be "pure punditry; many people use blogs to ask questions, to share news, or just to have conversations." And he makes another important point about blogging and reputation: "It's very important to be genuine when you blog, because the Internet does a good job of outing phoniness. The key to engaging on the Internet these days is to have a credible voice and respond to what's being said out there in an authentic way."

To draw visitors and keep them coming back to your blog, you have to offer content of value. Sometimes a blogger will report breaking news; "other times they are not so much scoops of fact, but what you might call scoops of perception," says Chris. A lot of opinions get created, shaped, or formed on blogs—so add your voice to the conversation and build your foreground reputation in the process.

No matter who you want to reach, no matter what you want to project, think before you post to your blog, comment on someone else's blog, write an online review, or upload a video. You want to be authentic, but how much is too much? Although I believe in spontaneity and authenticity, posting in the heat of the moment can be risky. If you're disrespectful or disclose inappropriately online, you can hurt your reputation (not to mention career or educational opportunities).

William Fitzsimmons, Dean of Admissions for Harvard University, tells me that he and his admissions people sometimes check applicants out on Facebook or MySpace or using Google. "Anything out there in the electronic world is public information," he explains. "If applicants put it out there on their own, it's in the public domain." Considering that Harvard receives 27,000 applications but accepts only 2,000 students a year, what the admissions staff sees on an applicant's blog or Facebook page can make a difference. Whether you're applying to Harvard, looking for a new job, or simply networking for the future, it pays to think before you post.

## Round Out Your Rep

Yet another key building block to round out your digital rep is a social networking profile. Join LinkedIn, Facebook, MySpace, Plaxo, and any other sites appropriate for your field or profession. I asked Elliot Schrage, Vice President of Communications for Facebook, exactly how this affects digital rep, and he said: "You build your reputation based on the information you share, the community you build, the information you react to, and your engagement in the communities where you choose to participate."

At LinkedIn, which is designed to encourage professional connections, you establish a profile and invite connections with people who are likely—or able—to recommend you. These may be current or former colleagues, bosses, clients, suppliers, distributors, committee members, and so on. The people you link to will affect the way new contacts view you and your rep, so be selective about who you invite (and about whose invitations you accept).

Reid Hoffman uses his own profile as an example: He has about 1,800 connections. "These range from people I met at a conference and I had a lengthy dinner with to people I've worked with for years. They all know me well enough to be able to say something about me. My LinkedIn profile essentially recommends me as an investor and as a board member. If people Google me, my profile—like many LinkedIn profiles—is the top search result."

If you were trying to evaluate Reid's background reputation, for example, you might look at his LinkedIn profile, see what he's involved in, and see who recommends him. Does someone you know also know him? "You can use the online reputation to assess who you want to check out," Reid tells me, "and get introduced through your trusted connection, which then gives you a chance of getting a very honest reference."

There's one more point I need to make right here: When you sign up on one of these sites, use your real name. Google might find your nickname, but is that the way to build your personal reputation?

# You're the Expert

Barbara Rozgonyi, the managing editor at wiredPRworks, suggests ten ways to become a recognized subject matter expert by participating in LinkedIn:

1. Grow your connections in the categories you want to reach; review every invitation before you accept to see if there's a fit with your profile.

2. After you accept an invitation, reply with a quick personal message that includes a few bullet points about what you do, an opportunity to ask questions about your industry, and additional ways to connect with you online such as your blog, e-zine, or forum.

3. Present your profile with benefits or accomplishments that highlight your expertise to your targeted audience.

4. In the web sites section of your profile, add a link to a page that lists your news, social media bio, articles, or publications.

5. In the answers area, post questions that collect information for a report or survey you'll publish as a white paper based on your LinkedIn community experience.

6. Answer relevant questions with specific information based on your expertise and work your way up to becoming an expert by giving top-rated answers.

7. Match your industries to your network, unless you're a consultant to a specific industry who will benefit from being visible to your peers as well as your consulting base.

8. Talk about your LinkedIn networking experiences on your blog and in your marketing communications.

9. Get recommended as an expert resource by asking those who value your insights to write a reference that promotes you (and them).

10. Redirect interest to your own personal community, such as a blog or forum, where people can learn, contribute, and continue

the dialogue with a link to, or mention of, the community in your public profile; track traffic to measure results.[5]

## Go to Their Party

You've set up your own web site, blog, and social networking profile(s). Now you can enhance your digital rep by getting involved in the e-communities and sites that are most important to your company, industry, or occupation. Where do authorities in your industry or profession blog, make guest "appearances," or comment? Where do colleagues and senior people look for professional advice or new insights? Which destinations draw the liveliest interactions? These are the online places to build your reputation by adding to the conversation.

Your list should target all of the well-populated social media networks, news sites, blogs, and forums. Be not only niche-specific but location-specific, because it pays to know people in the same profession who live or work in your city or area. You can do this research on Google and blog directories like Technorati, which will find blogs that cover your topic.

A couple of key points to note when you participate in these communities: Use the same name. It allows you to carry the trust you've built in one community to another. It makes it easier for people to find and befriend you, especially if you participate in multiple web sites. There's the additional benefit of reputation management; if you use the same name consistently, you'll increase your visibility on search engine results pages.

Specialize in your topics. Define your online persona by aligning yourself with topics or areas for which you want to be known as an expert or authority. For instance, submit stories, observations, or opinions in a specific field (business, marketing, science, health, software, your choice). On social networking sites like Facebook and MySpace, identify and befriend users with interests that fit your profession or industry focus. Associating your name with a specific field will develop your reputation as an enthusiast and eventually as an expert.

Send traffic back to your web site or blog. Include a link to your web site on all the profile pages for all the communities you've joined. But don't spam the communities you visit with your links. Engage in conversations and offer value by answering other users' questions. You can expound on issues raised elsewhere in your blog and drop a reference to your site only when it's relevant. Practice self-promotion sparingly; you don't want to be seen as a salesperson at a social gathering. Once you reach a certain level of trust within the community, people will reference you automatically. Links on these communities are usually permanent and they'll be long-term sources of steady traffic, particularly if the community is well populated.

Although you should spend the most time on communities, you should also build relationships away from communities. Each community you use serves as a means to not only build relationships with others of similar interests but also with influencers—people with an established reputation and a high level of trust within the specific industry or field. At this point, you can get off the computer and use the phone or personal meetings to continue building your relationship.

Don't let communities define and regulate how you interact with another individual. Sometimes they can limit the depth of any possible conversation. For instance, instead of reaching out to a blogger through a comment form, try establishing e-mail, instant messenger, or Twitter contact because you can form stronger bonds through them. When you participate in these communities, you should start to see recommendations by other members as your reputation builds.[6]

## Your 24/7 Rep

If your reputation isn't what you'd like, you'll need a plan to earn it back. One option, especially for a severely damaged reputation, is to pay a company like ReputationDefender to handle the repairs. I'll talk more about responding to negative online comments in Chapter 11, but for now, let me say that proactively managing your reputation is the best defense.

Use the spaces you control (your web page, your blog, your social networking profiles) to make a 24/7 positive impression. Play well with others by linking to authoritative or well-known bloggers that have a natural connection with your personal or professional interests. Contribute to online conversations without hogging the screen, sounding too full of yourself, or going on the attack. Keep your blog, web page, and profiles updated. Add social networking connections steadily yet judiciously.

This is a process, not a one-time task. Continue monitoring your digital rep. Spend time every week on your blog. Read and comment on other people's posts. Participate in the communities. Build your social network. I suspect the two traps here are (a) you set everything up and don't get back to anything for six months or (b) you get so sucked into the challenges and rewards that you spend time on the computer that should be spent on your job, career, and family. My advice: Maintain a balance and keep your eyes on the prize, a great rep.

Explore new and different ways to project yourself online and polish your foreground rep while adding to your background reputation. One example is Naymz.com, which says on its site: "Our philosophy is unique: A good professional reputation is the key to effectively networking with other professionals." Naymz allows you to create a profile and link it to your other social networking profiles; create a .name web address that points to your web profile (such as http://firstName .lastName.name); and create shortcut web addresses to your other profiles. Keep looking—I'm sure you'll find additional sites of value to your rep-enhancement plan.

And if you're building a small business? I'll talk about the tools and techniques available to build digital rep for small (and not-so-small) businesses in Chapter 8.

# Can a Small Business Build a Big Digital Reputation?

O f course it can. Think of Blendtec, which virtually built an entire consumer business on Internet videos shown on its WillItBlend.com web site and on YouTube.

Or think of formerly small businesses like Google, Facebook, and eBay that became big businesses on the strength of their digital reputations.

The real question is: *How* can a small business build a big digital reputation?

Peggy Wynne Borgman, the owner of Preston Wynne spas in Saratoga, California, realized she had to do something about her digital reputation when she discovered that four out of five reviewers on Yelp gave her a cold or lukewarm rating.

Yelp (at www.yelp.com) is an online urban city guide in which users rate places to eat, shop, drink, relax, and play. Yelp says it's different from traditional word-of-mouth in that it's "an easy and fun way for real locals to share opinions on the places they know and go." And of course it's on the Internet. Yelp extends the Amazon.com reviews model to restaurants, stores, bars, and more. It aspires to foster "a vibrant community of locals who feel connected both on Yelp and, gasp, in the real world," and to connect "the well-written and insightful reviews to the actual human beings who wrote them."

While Yelp encourages positive reviews of worthy businesses, it also wants to hear about bad experiences, as Peggy Borgman learned. To repair her small business's reputation, she used Yelp's e-mail system to write each critical reviewer to learn what had gone wrong and to try to make it right. She sent a thank-you note to the happy customer. She added a note to her e-mail newsletter that encouraged regular clients to go online and share their good experiences. As *The Wall Street Journal* reported, several months later, Borgman's spas' rating had climbed to an acceptable four stars.

"It's personal and it's painful, a public flogging like that," she says. Today, however, Yelp is an important source of visitors to her two spas, "which is funny, considering I originally thought it was the tool of the devil."[1]

## The Good, the Bad, and the Ugly

One more time: People are going to talk about your business whether you like it or not. They are going to be telling Yelp, Amazon, Zagat, Angie's List, TripAdvisor, Urbanspoon, Sazze, Edmunds, and dozens more customer feedback sites what they think of your service, your product, your quality, and your value. It's these comments, over which you have no control, that shape the opinion of people who know nothing else about you—your prospective customers, employees, suppliers, creditors, and anyone else who touches your business. As far as these stakeholders are concerned, these comments *are* your reputation.

What makes it especially personal and painful for the small business owner is that the unhappy customer is more likely to vent online than is the happy customer. "The conventional wisdom is that a satisfied customer will tell one person and an unhappy person will tell 10," says Clay Shirky, author of *Here Comes Everybody* and an expert on the reputation economy. "That's now been upped by orders of magnitude."[2]

As someone Yelped about a dry cleaner: "Do not go there!!! Just wasting your money and they will ruin your clothes. They made the stain on my cotton blouse BIGGER and also in more places. It also went through from the front to the back."

About an auto body shop: "Don't be fooled by the name change . . . I only post these reviews because I had SUCH a bad experience. Not only did they NOT fix my car, the service and owners were incredibly insulting and rude. I have never been yelled at before by a vendor but these guys took the cake for my first time."

About a child care service: "We tried to use this agency. We were very clear about the type of person we were looking for. They sent us only 1 application that was even close to what we asked for. We are in the northeast and they sent us several applicants who did not want to live in cold weather. When we asked for our application fee back they flatly refused. We informed them we would post honest reviews of the company wherever we could, they then called and threatened us." What kind of reputation are you building when a customer says you not only don't provide a service but also threaten reprisals if the customer goes online to complain?

Perhaps more distressing to companies that get slammed online is the knowledge that "a person like me" is the most credible source of information, according to the Edelman Trust Barometer, an annual survey by the Edelman public relations firm. More and more people trust a stranger's opinion over an expert's opinion and certainly over a company executive's opinion. "We have reached an important juncture, where the lack of trust in established institutions and figures of authority has motivated people to trust their peers as the best sources of information about a company," Edelman's CEO, Richard Edelman, said when he first observed this phenomenon a few years ago.

Edelman went on to say, "Companies need to move away from sole reliance on top-down messages delivered to elites toward fostering peer-to-peer dialogue among consumers and employees, activating a company's most credible advocates."[3] I suspect this applies more to large corporations than to relatively small businesses where the owner *is* the business and can speak naturally, authentically, and confidently about it. In the case of small businesses, the owners can, like Peggy Wynne Borgman, do something personally (and quickly) to address customers' complaints.

## Acknowledge the Negative, Accentuate the Positive

World 2.0 means that some disgruntled character—a customer, an employee, a competitor, a former friend or associate, an ex-girlfriend, an ex-boyfriend—can easily post information that could hurt your business. As I wrote in Chapter 1, Chick Edwards, the Washington state developer, learned the hard way that such material can very well dominate your search results.

Worse, the negative tends to be reinforced, because if people see something negative about you on the Internet, they avoid you or they pile on. For a small business, "it's better to try to dominate your results with positive information," says Michael Fertik, the CEO of ReputationDefender, a company that sells online reputation management services. "I would advocate that the best thing to do is to give yourself what we call Google insurance. Get in front of the problem and establish a positive reputation on the Internet before you get attacked. In this case, prevention is the best medicine."

How, exactly, can a business do that? Michael tells me: "You make sure that your happy customers and your employees all talk about you and your company on the Internet. You set up a testimonials web site. You set up a reviews web site. And you make sure your happy customers (not just the unhappy ones) go to the places where your company will be reviewed." As one Yelper from San Diego said about a Connecticut diner, "The food is perfect. I've never ordered anything here that wasn't exactly what it claimed to be and wasn't delicious . . . The staff can be iffy sometimes, but this place is normally packed, so give them a break, they're just doing their job."

Remember that transparency and trust are vitally important. As Michael says, "You need to go on the Web and encourage your customers to go on the Web, and create buffer zones of good, positive, fresh, truthful content." The key word here is "truthful." If a comment or review stinks of spin or puffery, it will do more damage than good. So don't have a friend—or a spouse—dropping boilerplate compliments right and left. You may get bounced off the site entirely.

In 2008, *Fast Company* reports, "a clutch of members of a Silicon Valley women's networking group were banned from Yelp. CEO

Jeremy Stoppelman says the networkers had a 'you review me, I review you' arrangement, which violates Yelp's terms. Adryenn Ashley, one of the deleted, denies it. She promptly registered the site Yelp-sucks .com and recruited some 200 business owners for a potential class-action lawsuit, alleging "their incomes were hurt and freedom of speech infringed."[4]

Even the best managed businesses have unhappy customers. Some may be totally unreasonable in their demands and impossible to satisfy (these are the ones you're happy to "lose" to a competitor) but some have legitimate complaints. You couldn't get the stain out of the blouse. The new waitress screwed up dinner orders. The mechanic didn't properly tighten a nut. The warehouse shipped the wrong item. People make mistakes.

In a perfect world, these unhappy customers will tell you that you screwed up and you'll be able to make amends—and continue to build a positive reputation—without it going further. In *this* world, however, some unhappy customers will say nothing to you but vent on the Internet. Others may tell you that you screwed up—like the lady unhappy with the child care agency—and *still* go online. You may have a thousand happy customers and ten unhappy ones; you might find you deserve the negative feedback that five of those ten give you.

There's a good business reason to listen to complaints and do your best to correct any missteps: It's an investment in your digital rep that can pay back many times over. Academics call it the "recovery paradox." Customers who complain of poor service are more delighted by the company's recovery from the lapse (and more complimentary about it) than they are by error-free service.[5] And they'll praise you all the more loudly because you fixed the problem.

I recommend you start with the assumption that something can always go wrong. Have a plan in place for receiving and addressing complaints. Treat your customers (and vendors and employees) with respect and take their complaints seriously. You'll build more trust if you apologize when appropriate than if you deny a problem occurred or try to place the blame elsewhere. Be prepared to offer solutions that both you and your customers can live with. Then protect your reputation by following through on your solutions as quickly as possible.

Thanks to the recovery paradox, your loudest complainers could wind up as your most vocal advocates. Meanwhile, the positive comments you attracted over time will help protect your reputation. "Even the best business will have a negative comment or two on the Internet; it's inevitable," Michael explains. "But your customer base will understand you have a pretty good track record if there are two negative comments and ten positive comments."

Anyone who has shopped for a book on Amazon understands this intuitively. Two people may hate a book and ten people love it; you make a decision based on both the volume and the content of the reviews. The negative reviews may be more penetrating and persuasive than the ten positive comments . . . and you don't buy the book. Or the two negative reviews are obvious whack jobs, so you do buy the book. Most people do know how to read reviews, but it raises another issue.

"You want to encourage customers from different demographics to write about different features of their experience and write in different ways," says Michael, giving this example: "When I read a restaurant review in Zagats, I'm less concerned about ambiance than I am about food. My girlfriend is more concerned about ambiance than she is about service. Different people care about different things. You want to get as many people as possible who have different tastes to invest a little time to contribute."

Ideally, you should have a mechanism to capture customer comments during or after a transaction—perhaps set up a laptop at the cashier's station so patrons can write and post brief reviews to your blog as they check out. Or distribute comment cards and scan the completed cards to post on your site or blog. Or have a monthly sweepstakes to capture e-mail addresses (making it clear that you want the addresses for follow-up communication).

Another approach is to survey customers informally about their satisfaction. Maintain a careful customer count and publish the percentage of the total who said they were satisfied. When a customer isn't satisfied, ask why and do something about it. "It's worth investing in that effort," says Michael, "because small business owners spend as much as 20 percent of the budget on some form of marketing, such as advertising or coupons or Google ad words. But if you're not aware of the impact of the Internet, you're losing your business."

# Permission and Reputation

For another take on ways to build your digital reputation, I talked to Gail Goodman, the president and CEO of Constant Contact. The company helps small businesses, associations, and nonprofit organizations connect with customers, clients, and members through e-mail marketing and online survey tools.

"E-mail is a permission-based medium, so it's actually all about reputation," Gail observes. "If you don't have a good reputation, you won't get permission to develop the dialogue with your customers. They have to trust you to grant you their e-mail address. It's a gift they can take back if you don't treat it with the respect it deserves."

On the other hand, Gail's experience shows that if you violate the customer's trust, or overcommunicate, or communicate only about your company—"what I call always asking for the order and never offering anything of value"—you'll destroy your reputation. You'll lose your permission privileges because people will either unsubscribe or, worse, mark your e-mail as spam. So think of e-mail as a very direct way to get feedback from your stakeholders—either they like (or at least accept) what you send them or they cut you off.

As an example of how to use e-mail to build your reputation and your business, take a look at Girls Learn to Ride (GLTR), which offers snowboarding, skateboarding, and surfing clinics for girls (and now women). Founder Mark Sperling came up with the idea after he tried to teach his then-girlfriend to snowboard. It didn't go well. He talked to friends who'd had the same experience—girls and young women wanted to learn but they needed a neutral instructor. He turned the idea into a successful business, and today GLTR promotes more than 700 extreme sports clinics and camps every year.

Although the company has used radio, TV, magazine advertising, and direct mail as well as pages on Facebook and MySpace to stay in touch with prospects and customers, Sperling says that e-mail is most effective. GLTR requests information about a girl's age, region, and sport when she joins the e-mail list or registers for one of the company's clinics or camps. With this opt-in permission, the firm can segment by region or sport and prepare messages (such as announcements of upcoming events) tailored to particular groups.

GLTR distributes a monthly e-mail newsletter with links to its web site (www.girlslearntoride.com), where it hosts an online magazine for the core audience of young women 14 to 25 years old. "The newsletter offers teasers about information on the web site, and we also include links to articles about music, popular female athletes, health, and other areas of interest," says Sperling.

Ultimately, GLTR's web site and e-mails do seek to sell the company's services—but they also help the company earn and spread its reputation by offering information, news, and entertainment valued by its audiences. The list started with 250 names and grew to over 10,000 names in just five years, demonstrating the reputational power of permission to e-communicate. "We track all of our participants and have found that more than 53 percent of them found out about us through the Internet or our e-mail newsletter," Sperling says.

## Opt In, Opt Out

Building the reputation of a small business with e-mail, of course, has its own pitfalls. You want to make it easy for people to join your list, and just as easy to get off it, and not just because the law requires you to tell people how to stop unwanted e-mail. Simply put, you don't want to be perceived as a spammer, let alone attract the Federal Trade Commission's attention (even inadvertently), if you want to maintain a sterling reputation.

Ideally, you should offer a one-click way for recipients to subscribe and, if they choose, unsubscribe. This is where it's helpful to think like a recipient. Gail Goodman of Constant Contact tells me: "I definitely have a negative reputation reaction when someone makes me work to get off their list. You click the bottom e-mail and then it makes you reenter your e-mail address. But you know my e-mail; you just sent me one. It's really important that you make it incredibly easy for people to get on and incredibly easy for people to get off your list."

In fact, the "unsubscribe" feature can actually act as a reputation thermometer. You know you have a reputation problem when you suddenly see a flood of "unsubscribe" notices. E-mail gives you instant feedback if you analyze the percentage of recipients who open the message and how often they forward your message. Track your numbers over time and you'll get a fascinating picture of your reputation among people who, at one time, thought highly enough of your firm to gift you with their e-mail address.

I asked Gail what she saw as the biggest problem with small and medium businesses in building their reputations in a digital world. Here's her answer: "Their biggest problem is that they don't know how to create a digital reputation. They don't understand that their reputation is important and fragile. They're so hungry for new business that they're willing to do just about anything."

Gail calls this the naïve marketer problem. "They don't know what's okay and what's not okay," she tells me. "Unfortunately, the online social media space has a lot of unwritten rules in terms of protocol, what's acceptable and what's not." So, for example, businesses should resist the urge to swap lists with other businesses. Remember, e-mail is a permission-based medium, and the people on the swapped list haven't given their permission to use their names in this way. Violate their trust, and you'll tarnish your digital rep.

## Will They Refer?

You can also monitor your business reputation through surveys sent to customers and prospects who have given you permission to send e-mail. One measure is the "Net Promoter Score" based on the question: How likely are you to refer this company to a friend or colleague?

Fred Reichheld discusses the Net Promoter Score in his book, *The Ultimate Question,*[6] in which he states that customer satisfaction is more important than any business criterion except profits. Reichheld argues that customer satisfaction is best measured by one question: "Would you recommend this business to a friend?" In other words, what is this business's reputation?

Pressure for financial performance, says Reichheld, tempts executives to seek "bad profits," profits obtained at the expense of frustrating or disappointing customers. Only relentless focus on customer satisfaction can generate "good profits."

Although not everyone is convinced by Reichhold's argument, it seems to me that, for many small businesses, asking the question can be a rough measure of what customers think of your business. If they're not comfortable recommending you, that suggests they don't have a very positive view of your reputation. If they would recommend you, it's one more deposit toward your reputation equity.

## KISS Your Site and E-Mails

Finally, because your web site and e-mails affect your reputation, let me offer a bit of advice. Keep your sites and messages appealing and interesting, yet simple to navigate. Be sure visitors can locate the information or products they want quickly and with as few clicks as possible. Include lots of details and keep your messages, web pages, and blogs updated so visitors can both recognize their needs and identify solutions.

Be transparent about who you are and how to contact you. Build trust through full disclosure of pricing, shipping charges, refunds, returns, and privacy policies. Invite visitors to opt in to ongoing e-mail communications and provide an easy way for them to opt out if they choose (but do consider asking why they want to opt out). Include links in your e-mails to bring visitors back to see new online content again and again. And don't forget to save room for user reviews or comments.

I'll leave the last word to Gail: "The wonderful thing about e-mail as a medium is that people who join your mailing list are the most likely to know other people like themselves. If they're interested in what you do, they probably know five other people who are also interested in what you do. If you add value for them, they will share with others and spread your reputation very inexpensively."

Once you become a big business, how can you build a correspondingly big reputation? I'll discuss that in the next chapter.

# Big Business, Big Digital Rep

You may not have heard of Bill Heard Enterprises, but the corporation, with $2.5 billion in annual revenue, allowed its reputation to deteriorate to such an extent that the company collapsed in September 2008.

At the height of its success, Bill Heard employed 2,700 people, owned 15 automobile dealerships in seven states from Arizona to Florida, and was the country's 11th largest Chevrolet dealer group. General Motors named it one of its "Dealers of the Year" in 2005. Heard clearly had to be doing something right for years—Bill Heard Sr. began selling cars in 1919—to have grown to that size.

But behind the scenes, something must have been going wrong. In recent years, Better Business Bureaus in seven states received more than 500 complaints against the company. The president of the BBB of Greater Houston told *Automotive News* that Bill Heard stores there "are the most complaint-ridden dealerships in our files." At one point, a BBB staff member in Nashville was assigned full-time to handle complaints against the local Heard dealership.

The Georgia Governor's Office of Consumer Affairs cited Heard dealerships 15 times from 1991 to 2007 for violating the state's Fair Business Practices Act. Georgia sued the company in 2007 after Heard sent 10,000 car owners an "urgent potential recall notice" that appeared to come from GM. The lawsuit alleged the company was trying to make consumers think their cars were unsafe when, in fact, it actually wanted to sell them new cars or service plans. According to media reports, Heard had paid $280,000 in fines and penalties in Georgia, $183,000 in Tennessee, and $400,000 in Florida in the past few years.

True, Bill Heard Enterprises had more problems than its reputation. The company's own statement announcing the closure of its dealerships blamed "rising fuel prices, a product portfolio of mostly heavy trucks and sport utility vehicles, economic recession, unfavorable local market conditions for vehicle sales, the crisis in the banking and financing sectors."

I'm sure those were all contributing factors in the company's downfall. Yet reputation was likely an issue as well, according to Cliff Banks on WardsAuto.com: "Perhaps it was rogue employees or a culture within the group that allowed or even encouraged questionable behavior. Whatever the case, the Heard group was unable to shake the perception that it conducted business unethically."

In turn, Banks observed, this led to a very serious problem: "GMAC Financial Services stopped financing the inventory for several of Bill Heard's stores, hampering the group's ability to floor plan and order vehicles. Heard apparently was unable to secure financing from other sources. That inability to obtain credit ultimately forced the group to shut down business operations. GMAC will not say why it pulled the plug on Heard, but it could have been because it was not happy with the company's deteriorating reputation and that likely played into the finance firm's decision."[1]

## Reputation Takes on a Life of Its Own

The Heard situation may be an extreme case, but it illustrates my key point: You can't afford to ignore your corporate reputation because it takes on a life of its own. Heard's corporate web site continued to feature a notice about auctioning off assets months after the company's demise. That was the official message. When I did a quick search in early 2009, I found more than 700,000 results—opinions, articles, and commentary about Heard on blogs, news sites, and other places online. Heard's reputation lives on.

Because a large corporation touches so many more stakeholders than an individual or a small business, its task in establishing and maintaining a positive digital reputation is more complex and far-reaching. The basic principles for reputation-building outlined in Chapters 7 and 8 still apply, but on a larger scale. With greater resources, a corporation has more possibilities for enhancing its digital reputation, for starting and maintaining an online dialogue—including full color, sound and video web presences where stakeholders can hold conversations, learn, and be entertained.

My colleagues and I have found that many senior corporate executives don't understand how much of a voice the average citizen now has in the most pressing issues of the day. Given the political, economic, and social climate in which we live, people *want* to have a voice. They're struggling to express their frustrations, but they also want to communicate their ideas—and that presents opportunity for your business.

We frequently meet senior executives who say they want to understand what conversations are currently taking place before they commit to doing anything about their firm's digital rep. Actually, this is the monitoring step I described in Chapter 2; it should lead to specific recommendations about what management ought to be saying and how the company ought to be engaging with various stakeholders. So far, so good.

The problem is that the conventional white-shirt-and-power-tie crowd that governs many corporate executive suites wants to control the message. Yet building a corporate digital rep is nothing like running an advertising campaign. The company can control its ads; it can't control what is being said about it online or where someone says it. Dialogues among and between your stakeholders are going to occur with or without your company's input or participation. Customers are going to blog or tweet or post messages about happy and unhappy experiences with you, your sales people, your dealers, your products, your services, and your financial policies.

If you can't control the message or the media, what can you do? You can engage people in genuine conversations, address their complaints, solicit their suggestions, and provide news and information. If your company doesn't engage, you face the very real risk of having a small group of consumers, constituents, or activists define and shape your reputation— even if their viewpoint is negative, or inaccurate, or inappropriate.

## Wal-Mart Gets the Message

A few years ago, Wal-Mart's management seemed to have a hands-off approach to digital rep even as it was attacked online through sites such as the union-backed WakeUpWalMart.com. Then Wal-Mart decided to retake and reshape its reputation, as *BusinessWeek* reported in 2006: "The Bentonville (Ark.)-based company has been pushing hard to improve its public image, at a time when its financial fortunes increasingly depend on it. It's come under heavy fire from workers and politicians, for everything from the low wages it pays workers to the small retailers it pushes out of business. That dark reputation has resulted in communities around the country taking on Wal-Mart, by trying to halt construction of new stores or forcing it to pay higher wages and benefits."[2]

Trying to improve the retailer's digital rep and control some of the online conversation, Wal-Mart's PR agency set up Working Families for Wal-Mart and was behind a fake blog called "Wal-Marting Across America." The fake blog backfired and gave Wal-Mart a black eye in the blogosphere. Wal-Mart got the message.

Since that false start, the retailer has become committed to facilitating online conversations in a big way. First it introduced the Checkout Blog (http://checkoutblog.com/), where in-house experts comment about products, packaging, and everything else under the Wal-Mart sun. "It puts real personality out there in a real conversation," says Nick Agarwal, who helped introduce the blog. Especially when the bloggers don't have to parrot the company line: "Readers can tell if people are being genuine or monitored," says Wal-Mart merchandise manager Alex Cook, who blogs about gadgets.[3]

Over time, Wal-Mart has expanded its web site to draw visitors into an ever-growing number of conversations. A few examples: the Baby Buzz Blog, free classified ads posted by customers, customer-authored product reviews, and general customer comments on everything from healthy living to football rankings. These online dialogues are not only starting to engage stakeholders and to demonstrate the retailer's new transparency, they're helping Wal-Mart to turn its digital rep around.

## Sony Shines Online

Unlike Wal-Mart's spotty rep, Sony has long had a positive reputation, offline as well as online. That's why I asked Rick Clancy, senior vice president for corporate communications at the U.S. headquarters of Sony Electronics Inc., to talk about how his company engages stakeholders to support its digital rep. With annual North American sales of about $12 billion, Sony Electronics has a wide range of stakeholders to reach, including consumers, professional and business customers, dealers and resellers, investors, employees, suppliers, business partners, members of the media, the creative community, and government officials.

"The reputation of Sony relates to the company's credibility, the trustworthiness, and the degree of confidence that different stakeholder groups have in Sony, be they investors or consumers or others, even our employees," Rick tells me. "Both the corporate reputation and the brand image are critical in terms of sustaining our premium position in the marketplace."

Sony's brand barometer and its net promoter score are two indicators of where the company stands with U.S. consumers, a key external audience. Sony's employee surveys show how the internal audience views the company, its values, and its vision. Coming soon is an employee communications social networking platform to encourage idea exchange and conversations among the entire workforce.

Then there's Sony's digital rep strategy, which uses the company's unique strengths to differentiate itself as an innovator, an environmentallyconscious corporate citizen, and a customer-focused firm. One of the first initiatives was a blog Rick started in mid-2007 (http://news.sel.sony.com/electronicsblog/). "Conversations were occurring anyway in forums we did not control and we were not very engaged in," says Rick.

Now the blog puts a human face on Sony and provides a specific forum for stakeholder conversations. In fact, reader comments are very lightly moderated: "Positive, negative, critical—we take all comments, unless there are obscenities or the comments are totally off topic," Rick explains. "And it's very apparent to me every day that you have a thick skin in all of this."

Earlier this year, Rick's blog was folded into a broader Sony Electronics community site, which serves as a gateway to four e-communities: Digital Darkroom, all about digital photography; Frontline, which invites participation in online surveys, panels, and other Sony research; Voice Your Opinion, where visitors can post reviews of Sony products; and Backstage 101, the Online Learning Center (more about that in a moment). The umbrella site also includes links to the company's online presence in Facebook, Flickr, YouTube, and Twitter, plus videos and podcasts hosted by different Sony experts and downloads of Sony product images and ads.

The candid nature of online reader comments and reactions has strengthened the partnership between Rick's corporate communication team and their colleagues in customer service, product development and design, engineering, marketing, and sales: "We are now looking at consumer feedback—whatever its nature—as an opportunity to satisfy our customers, one at a time. Whether it is information, product support, repair, or servicing—each of these situations is an opportunity to win back customer loyalty, trust, and confidence."

I want to single out Sony's Online Learning Community (http://backstage101.learningcenter.sony.us/index.jsp) because it's a good example of giving people something to talk about and a place to talk about it. This site offers dozens of free online tutorials, courses, and forums covering the basics of personal computing, home entertainment technology, digital photography, and digital video. Newbies and experienced users alike can browse course descriptions about topics such as how to set up a wireless home network and how to shoot better home videos, then check user reviews and read the instructor's bio before they click to enroll for free. Entire courses can be downloaded in .pdf format for review and reference, and instructors respond quickly to users' questions and comments. The quality is high, the instructors are professional, the discussion is helpful, and the entire experience adds up to a big plus for Sony's digital rep and its brand image.

Rick has another interesting observation that may be tied to the effect of World 2.0 and building a reputation. As a result of the various online initiatives, people at Sony Electronics are becoming even more sensitive to customers and their experience with the company—and are doing what they can to improve that experience. Being in corporate communications, for example, many of Rick's interactions have been with journalists, industry analysts, or government representatives; he traditionally had little contact with the customers who actually use Sony's products. "Now I have this terrific opportunity to put the 'public' back into public relations," he tells me. "We still have to deal through filters like reporters, but now there's this opportunity to have a dialogue directly with consumers."

Showing a human face behind the faceless corporation can only build reputation equity, a vital asset for any corporation (assuming it's a responsive, helpful, authentic face). And this brings me back to moral purpose, which I mentioned in Chapter 4.

## Know Your Moral Purpose

Even a public company that has a financial responsibility to its shareholders can and should have moral purpose that it can clearly articulate to customers, employees, and other stakeholders. In my view, your reputation grows out of your moral purpose. Let me quote Edward Kopko, CEO of the global engineering and IT firm Butler International: "The higher moral purpose of a business organization and the people who make it go is to first serve the community of users of their products and services. To provide a needed service, at a lower cost, with better technology, is my definition of a moral purpose."

He adds, "Think of health care and how the life expectancy of many millions of people has been dramatically extended in recent times. We are by definition better off when we exchange our services and trade with each other. Too many companies and CEOs feel apologetic for running a successful, profitable company. This is hard to understand. CEOs should see their success as an asset to the community. If they choose to support the community in some additional philanthropic or charitable way, that should not be viewed as the basis for their moral purpose. Charity and philanthropy are things we all should be doing, of course. But a well-run successful business has a high moral purpose by definition."[4]

Butler International's web site lists the company's seven values as: (1) being the best; (2) lifelong learning; (3) innovation and creativity; (4) honesty and integrity; (5) embracing change; (6) having fun; and (7) improving our world. Without question, this is an unambiguous statement of the company's moral purpose. Yes, the company has to make a profit to remain in business, but its moral purpose goes beyond, wrapping around the workforce as well as the world.

Mark Fuller, the founder and chairman of Monitor Group, has a more expansive, and to my mind more persuasive, definition. He defines moral purpose as "a systematic set of unifying and energizing aspirations that guides its strategic vision and action. As manifested and enacted through current and past leadership behavior, policies, organizational structure, and writings, moral purpose makes the continued existence of that organization meaningful and significant to internal and external constituents. Moral purpose engages these constituencies, endows legitimacy, and creates competitive advantage." In other words, it's the higher calling an organization pursues that goes beyond the specific objective to make money.

Bill George, the former CEO of Medtronic, writes in his book, *Authentic Leadership: Rediscovering the Secrets to Creating Lasting Value,* "Over the last several decades, businesses have evolved from maximizing the physical output of their workers to engaging the minds of their employees. To excel in the twenty-first century, great companies will go one step further by engaging the hearts of their employees through a sense of purpose. When employees believe their work has a deeper purpose, their results will vastly exceed those who use only their minds and their bodies. This will become the company's competitive advantage."

George argues, and I agree, that it is only through a sense of purpose that companies can realize their potential. "It is their raison d'etre that animates employees and inspires them to turn purpose into reality. The authentic way to increase shareholder value is with a mission that inspires employees to create innovative products and provide superior service to customers. Product innovations and superior service translate into increased market share and expanded market opportunities, creating growth in revenues and the ability to sustain price levels. This is the basis for sustained competitive advantage, increased levels of profitability, and higher profit margins. Consistent profit growth forms the basis for sustained increases in shareholder value."[5]

Moral purpose motivates employees to create an advantage for the organization. It also supports and infuses a company's reputation with external stakeholders.

## Purpose Transcends Profit

What does all this have to do with your corporation's digital rep? In the absence of a clear (or clearly stated) moral purpose, the organization will fall back on expediency and will view profit as its sole reason for being. Maybe expedience as a driving force will work for a time, but it leaves management and employees without a long-term sense of purpose other than chasing the almighty buck. Once stakeholder relations are only a matter of dollars and cents, support will erode and your digital rep will be dinged.

People seek meaning in their lives, says Mark, and since they spend most of their time at work, they seek it in what they do. An organization that has a clear moral purpose is one in which employees, customers, suppliers, dealers, and neighbors prefer to associate. People want to buy—literally and figuratively—into a company's strong moral purpose. They're loyal to companies that have earned a reputation of embodying a worthwhile purpose.

Moral purpose is something you just can't fake. It is not a strategy or a mission statement. It can't be the management fad of the month. Companies that talk the talk but don't walk the walk of moral purpose will be exposed during periods of stress that demand heroism, innovation, excellence, and commitment to the greater good. On the other hand, if people know what you stand for and see you stand up for it during any crisis, you'll gain admirers and advocates who will praise you in blogs, reviews, and other conversations.

Mark argues that a real moral purpose has three characteristics.

1. It is enacted, not espoused. You can force people to sign statements of moral purpose (if they want to keep their jobs, they'll sign), but unless they truly understand and embody the purpose, it's a waste of time, ink, and paper.

2. It is integrated across many different functions so that employees in different departments—marketing, finance, human resources, customer service, operations, manufacturing, whatever—embrace the same moral purpose. Because it is integrated and departments do not work at cross purposes, it gives the organization an enormous competitive advantage.

3. It is competitively relevant. It does not simply make people feel good, it helps the organization thrive in good times and survive in bad.

A good case in point is Stonyfield Farm, the world's largest maker of organic yogurt. Just glance at its web site (http://stonyfieldfarm .com) and you'll see that the company is greener than the greenback—which is, in fact, why it inspires loyalty and enjoys a sterling reputation among people who care about that moral purpose. Although Stonyfield was bought by France's Groupe Danone a few years ago, the parent company has wisely avoided interfering with Stonyfield's strong commitment to its moral purpose.

Here's how CEO Gary Hirshberg describes that purpose in his book, *Stirring It Up*: "High on Stonyfield's agenda is our top priority—real wealth. As a business, we've pledged to do anything feasible to help reduce environmental costs and rebalance the planet's natural systems, from the land to the atmosphere." Combining moral purpose with profits meant "taking a gamble that a truly honest product—pure yogurt—would attract customers so in tune with our environmental goals that both our business and our ideals would flourish. The gamble paid off, but only after we made our mission clear to ourselves, our customers, our investors, and the world."[6]

Stonyfield's web presence reflects its moral purpose and its desire to maintain a real dialogue with stakeholders. The site describes its products in detail but also offers an e-mail newsletter (Moosletter, actually), a blog about life on a Vermont family organic farm, and educational information about organic foods, wellness, environmental issues, and more. Visitors are invited to get involved through advocacy, education, and living greener lives. They can also add their voices to the Stonyfield e-community discussion and provide feedback about products, causes, and so on. No wonder the subtitle of Hirshberg's book is *How to Make Money and Save the World.*

Of course, your company's moral purpose may have nothing to do with hugging trees (which could be categorized as altruism or heroism, depending on your perspective). Google's moral purpose, according to its mission statement, is "to organize the world's information and make it universally accessible and useful." Everything Google does, everything it communicates, relates to that moral purpose.

Johnson & Johnson consistently ranks high on *Fortune*'s list of America's Most Admired Companies, in part because its actions are guided by its famous credo, which says that the needs of customers, employees, and communities come before responsibilities to stockholders. J&J's web site explains: "Our Credo is more than just a moral compass. We believe it's a recipe for business success. The fact that Johnson & Johnson is one of only a handful of companies that have flourished through more than a century of change is proof of that."[7]

By the way, J&J has a blog, JNJ BTW (get it?), to host online conversations. The blog's description is: "By The Way . . . Everyone else is talking about our company, so why can't we? There are more than 120,000 people who work for Johnson & Johnson and its operating companies. We're some of them, and through JNJ BTW, we will try to find a voice that often gets lost in formal communications." And that's one way J&J polishes its digital rep. (The blog includes a message of apology from Kathy Widmer, VP of marketing for McNeil

Healthcare, about the Motrin commercial that inadvertently offended moms—see Chapter 5 for the full story.)

## Digital Rep Is an Ongoing Challenge

To build your company's digital reputation, you have to do the right thing, and you have to do it for a long time. You can't just build a reputation overnight. Once you've started to establish your digital rep, you can add to it, polish it, and bring out different facets. You can't be all things to all people, but your digital rep can reflect who you are and what you stand for in many ways. Keep your online dialogues going, talk about what your company is doing, invite conversation, listen to what stakeholders are saying all over the Web, and respond (with actions as well as words) accordingly.

Another challenge is that although you'll need top-level support, a CEO's tenure today is too short. A chief marketing officer's tenure is even shorter, about 22 months according to some authorities. As Beth Comstock, corporate senior vice president and chief marketing officer at General Electric, remarked to me, "That's barely time to get your bearings and get a plan going." Turnover at the top has become an issue for many reasons, but it adds yet another layer of complexity to the process of building a good digital rep with C-level support and involvement.

The good news is once you're set up to monitor who's saying what about you and actively engage with your stakeholders online, you've laid a solid foundation that transcends individual executives or employees. It's good to have internal people put a human face on your company—Rick Clancy and the employees who participate in Sony's e-communities add a real dash of personality to the actual content. But the company's entire digital rep doesn't (and shouldn't) hang on a single person.

That said, you still may want to put some of your people in the spotlight to boost the company's digital rep. Tom Dickson is the well-known CEO of Blendtec—well-known because he's starred in dozens of "Will It Blend?" YouTube videos, which have sold thousands of blenders for the company. Chapter 10 is all about the YouTube juggernaut.

# Tools and Tactics

# The YouTube Juggernaut

Here's how DeAndre Way, a teenager in Batesville, Mississippi, built his digital rep on YouTube.com and parlayed it into a successful business venture. Way happened upon YouTube while searching for cartoons on the Internet. "I was impressed with the idea that I could type almost anything in the search box and videos associated with it would pop out," he says. "So I started uploading videos of me promoting my music. Most of them were just me acting a fool, but in others I was acting like I was a real rapper—telling people my album was about to drop soon."

Way, who had been posting original music to Soundclick .com, adopted the stage name Soulja Boy Tell 'Em and began cross-promoting his videos on his Soundclick page and his music on YouTube. He then established a MySpace music page and a web site, Souljaboytellem.com, with links to YouTube and Soundclick. His music began to click.

"I was so famous on YouTube and MySpace that people started booking me for shows," says Soulja Boy. "Every time I did a show in a new city, people knew my songs. It showed me the true power of the Internet." In April 2007, he posted a homemade video of himself dancing to his song "Crank That" on YouTube. It became a viral hit; as of this writing it had been watched almost 20 million times.

That led to a record deal with Collipark Music/Interscope Records. "Crank That (Soulja Boy)" became the top-selling digital track in the U.S. in 2007. In all, it's sold 3.9 million digital downloads and the subsequent album "Souljaboytellem.com" sold more than 943,000 units. The rapper has also sold 2.4 million ringtone versions of "Crank That." He recently launched an online animated/live-action series, aiming to have a comedy network pick it up for TV.

But, Suzie Reider points out, it's not just his video posts that have built Soulja Boy's reputation. Suzie, hired as YouTube's chief marketing officer in 2006, notes that the rapper has an instructional video on YouTube that's been viewed almost 40 million times. "It's not just the dance he does. It's the 365-plus video responses to his video—by marching bands, ballet classes, aerobics classes. It's people who have put together Dora the Explorer and Happy Feet Penguins versions, different iterations of his dance uploaded as responses to his video." Not a bad reputation for a hip-hop crazy school kid who turned 18 in 2008—a reputation made possible, in large part, by the YouTube juggernaut.

Lots of businesses, large and small, are leveraging YouTube to polish their digital reps and connect with customers and others. Consider the social media savvy of the Detroit Red Wings hockey team, for instance. Its YouTube channel features player videos and fan comments (cheers and boos, I might add). It has a separate site, Red Wings TV, filled with videos of game highlights. It offers mobile phone updates and promotions; posts podcast player interviews; and provides branded widgets for fans to display on MySpace pages, Blogger blogs, and other sites. In short, the team is ready to continue fan conversations anywhere and everywhere, all year long.

## YouTube and Your Video Rep

YouTube, like the Internet itself, is unimaginably large. If YouTube were a country, it would be the third most populous in the world. With well over 300 million worldwide users, YouTube would rank behind only China and India.

YouTube is also a major search site, the second largest after Google (which owns it). When I checked ComScore not long ago, YouTube was logging some 2.6 billion searches per month, while Google had 7.6 billion. At that time, Yahoo had 2.4 billion searches, MySpace had nearly 600 million, and Facebook had nearly 200 million.

And these searchers have a lot of videos to search through. YouTube reports that over 13 *hours* of video are uploaded every minute and that in 2007 the site consumed as much bandwidth as the entire Internet in 2000.[1] Considering that YouTube went live (as they say in World 2.0) in February 2005, it's achieved an incredible record of growth in a very short time.

I have to believe a large part of YouTube's appeal is to the video-savvy next generation. When my family and I go on vacation, my two older teenagers take still pictures to post on their Facebook pages; their 12-year-old brother takes only videos, never still pictures. He videos himself, edits and laughs at his own videos, then exchanges videos with friends. In short, this new generation is highly focused on video communication—which is why YouTube, the largest of the video sites by far, will be at the core of everybody's video reputations for years to come.

## Paradigm of Showing and Sharing

One major reason for YouTube's popularity: You don't have to be a video wizard or post professional clips to participate. You don't even need a video camera; you can make a video with a cell phone, a computer, a digital camera, or a Flip camcorder. Because it's so cheap and easy to create and post video, anybody can be a reporter, an actor, or a commentator. Anybody can do something—sing and dance, give a speech, narrate a tour of the plant, show how a product is made, cheer a favorite politician—and put it on the Web.

And video is popular because the world is going visual. Visual communication has always had more impact than text, but we now have the ability to communicate visually worldwide at any moment. Other sites can provide video (Wikipedia listed 44 current U.S. video sharing web sites in January 2009), but they can't provide the community that's been built around YouTube. The phenomenon is not hard to understand, but where is it evolving and how is it influencing personal, professional, and corporate reputations on the Web?

Clearly, the power of showing and sharing—not telling and presenting—is a paradigm of YouTube. Soulja Boy's experience is just one example of how this works in the realm of personal digital rep. Video has also emerged as a powerful influence on corporate reps because people can show the world exactly what they think of your company—why they're unhappy or what they like—and they don't need your permission to do it.

YouTube's Suzie Reider told me about a vacationer to Aruba who posted an enthusiastic, well-done video tour of the resort hotel where he stayed. "The manager was so impressed and pleased that he invited the guest to return for another week, for free," she said. "The video actually gave a better sense of the experience of staying at this hotel than anything the resort's promotional team had come up with. It was completely authentic."

Point, shoot, and post means authentic, unsolicited, and personal video views of anything and everything. In fact, if you search for "hotels" on YouTube, you'll find more than 470,000 videos. Many have been posted by the hotels themselves. But thousands of other videos have been posted by travelers—some positive, some negative, and some in between. People take vacation videos and they want to show them. What better place than on YouTube?

The power of YouTube's show-and-share community has led to a new era of citizen journalism that can have a very serious, very speedy impact on your products, your service, and your reputation. After a U.S. Airways jet made an emergency landing in the Hudson River this past January, every TV news outlet ran a crawl asking viewers who took videos or photos to contact the station. Within 12 hours, viewers were able to watch consumer-generated footage of the actual crash and rescue efforts on YouTube and on news sites.

Even without a camera, people can touch off a YouTube stampede simply by tipping off the media. That's how the footage of rats in a New York City Taco Bell restaurant made the TV news and wound up on YouTube, where it's been viewed more than a million times and inspired a few video parodies, as well. The lack of control over what gets posted may strike fear into the hearts of some executives, but in reality, that's the great advantage of YouTube (as the Aruba hotel discovered, to its delight).

## The YouTube Universe

A YouTube video can, in some cases, have more impact on your reputation than a blog, because blog posts take time to discover and to read. Click to the YouTube home page and you'll see tabs for the most discussed, most viewed, favorite, and featured videos. It's quick and easy to search for videos on any subject or about any company—your firm as hero or villain, good corporate citizen, or uncaring employer.

The YouTube site is easy to navigate, with each video accompanied by links to related videos. For example, search results for "One Laptop Per Child" include a John Lennon video that was just made about giving a laptop to a Third World child. The screen has links to John Lennon's songs and to other nonprofits that might be similar. If I click on *Imagine*, I can watch that video and see links to John Lennon and some of his causes. Plus every video includes and invites viewer comments, adding to the community conversation. Clicking on any one of the video links brings up an entirely new network, a bit like a new solar system with its own planets and moons.

If you want to track a company's or an individual's reputation—yours or someone else's—spend some time studying and following the links to the solar systems that connect with your video starting point. Whether you're a big company, a small business, or an individual (like Sarah Palin or someone else with a high public profile), you'll see patterns in the connections of solar systems—both local and global links—that can profoundly influence your digital reputation.

The importance of these links will only increase in the coming years, as visual search and the visual presentation of content online become even more dominant than text-based communications. To make the most of video search opportunities, a company should establish its own YouTube channel so it can aggregate and organize its own material and not be completely subject to the YouTube algorithms that set up the network links.

## Your YouTube Channel

With a channel, you have one central place for posting video content about your people, your progress, and your products. PepsiCo, The March of Dimes, the NBA, Burger King, even the U.S. Senate and House of Representatives have their own YouTube channels, as do many members of the House and Senate. "The Royal Channel" is the YouTube home for videos concerning Britain's royal family, including Queen Elizabeth's 1957 Christmas message. The list goes on and on.

Of course you'll post your video content on your own web site, but YouTube is still an indispensable venue. With links back to your site and to other relevant videos, YouTube becomes an organized reputation management system that's part social—by inviting outside comment—and part creative. Although a YouTube video blown to fill an entire computer screen may not offer the sharpest picture, it's still pretty good, and the impact it can have on your reputation is powerful.

Companies should organize their visual material with their reputations in mind, recognizing they are building video libraries that will last a good long time. I asked Suzie Reider if YouTube videos are available forever. Her answer: "We don't really know what 'forever' means. Once you upload a video, it's in the system. It's going to stay up unless you, the user, take it down." Could I look back at my vacation video 25 years from now? "We sure hope so. There's certainly no plan for any of this video to disappear," she tells me.

## Getting Ready for YouTube and More

Large companies or nonprofits that want to build their reputations using YouTube should appoint a director of digital visual communication or digital visual content. This organizational role has two main areas of responsibility. One is to develop videos that show how the company produces its products, what makes them durable, functional, original, or all three. Where appropriate, these videos should cover how to use the product, how to repair it, even how to dispose of it (especially if environmental protection links back to the firm's moral purpose).

The second area of responsibility is to monitor and respond to user-generated video and content that others post on YouTube. These videos may be positive—the happy Aruba vacationer—or negative, neither of which you can control. (This means you have to be careful of your behavior, too, because videos are going to be everywhere.) The goal is to use the positives to the organization's benefit and to address the negatives with content that is thoughtful and direct.

Even if you don't have a director of digital visual communication, you must have monitors watching for user-generated video content and staff members who can ready a timely video response. I think Taco Bell waited a little too long to post its video response. It was a few days after the Taco Bell rats video popped up on YouTube before the president of US Yum Brands appeared in a video to apologize, explain what the firm was doing to prevent a recurrence, and reassure customers of Taco Bell's commitment to quality. He appeared in another update video a couple of days later, again apologizing and outlining specific steps the company had taken to resolve the issue.

Both videos are still posted in the news release section of Taco Bell's corporate web site and on YouTube. Judging by the number of views to date, neither corporate video approached the wide circulation of the rat video. It's difficult to know whether a faster video response would have quelled the furor, but at least Yum Brands would have had its say and its video would have been linked to the rat footage for viewers to find from the very start.

## Video-Oriented Culture

This leads to another key point: Every organization needs a more video-oriented culture to thrive in World 2.0. We're not going back to the text-based culture of the pre-YouTube era. So instead of an employee newsletter distributed through interoffice mail, how about a video newsletter that employees can watch on mobile devices or laptops? If you want, upload videos to YouTube and restrict access to those on your internal list, which is easy to do. Or establish a private, password-protected video section on your employee, supplier, or dealer web site for internal communications.

You also need a highly visual component in all your external communications. Why not do a visual annual report and release it on YouTube as part of its distribution? Send it to your stockholders first and tell them where to find more on your YouTube channel.

Greater visual communication gives you a chance to humanize your company and connect with your stakeholders. Your position can no longer be something like: "We are the company. We know best. We are going to control our image and our reputation. We will let you have the information we think you should have."

Now, rather than a monologue, you can use visual communication to start dialogues with your stakeholders—and you can show those conversations actually taking place. This allows you to start weaving together all of the information that influences your corporate reputation and to showcase activities that affect your position in the marketplace. Creating a library of all this material builds a forward momentum around what you're about and what you stand for. If you're open, honest, and creative about the content you create, it will start to affect the user-generated content (positive and negative) you can't control.

## Involve Your Customers

If you want to tap outside creativity, jump-start a digital dialogue, and build a reputation as a video-savvy company, you should engage and involve customers on YouTube. Here's a good example. SanDisk Corporation, which makes memory cards for cameras, held a YouTube contest called the SanDisk Point & Shoot Film Festival. It invited consumers to submit videos taken with point-and-shoot digital cameras in any of five categories (Kid Moves, Pet Moves, Dance Moves, Action Moves, and Comedy Moves). The top 200 entrants received a large-capacity SanDisk card; the category winners received cash prizes; the grand prize-winner received cash and a trip to Las Vegas. SanDisk still shows the top videos on its YouTube channel.

Some companies prefer to host video contests on their own web sites with links to and from YouTube. Heinz has twice invited customers to make their own Heinz ketchup TV commercial and submit it to the company's "Top This TV" site. The second time, Heinz posted information and updates (in video and text form) on its YouTube channel, along with links to the company-sponsored contest site. After the votes were counted, Heinz posted the winning video on its YouTube channel as well as on its contest site. By now, Heinz's "Top This TV" YouTube channel has been viewed nearly 300,000 times and the materials are all part of Heinz's video library.

Video contests have become so popular, in fact, that a web site (www.vidopp.com) now tracks them and updates the list of online video competitions every day. The VidOpp editor studies contest rules to report judging criteria, any costs involved, and any exploitation or scam risks. VidOpp says that it posted $2.6 million worth of cash contests in 2008. If you're going to run a video contest, let these people know about it.

So many companies are jumping on the YouTube bandwagon that *The Onion* has even posted a video satire titled "YouTube Contest Challenges Users to Make A 'Good' Video." Here's the text description of this fake news clip: "YouTube is offering a cash prize to the first user to upload a video with a shred of originality or artistic merit."

But seriously, your YouTube channel can help you tap the creativity of the people who care most about your organization, cause, or activity. As a consumer, if you enjoyed your experience at Disney World, Six Flags, or Myrtle Beach, would you do a short video of it? I suspect many, many people are filming videos of their kids at Disney World that, with just a little editing, would be very cute and would be a nice addition to the park's digital reputation if they were available on YouTube.

## Viewers Will Take You Viral

How can you get people to view the videos you'd like them to see? As I said in Chapter 5, it all starts with content. The only reason someone will watch is if there is a value exchange, and the value exchange in video is the content. Is it funny, poignant, interesting, informative, entertaining, engaging, whatever? Ask not what the video does for the organization, ask what it does for the viewer. If you don't design content for your particular target audiences (consumers, suppliers, employees, distributors, and so on), they won't watch.

By the way, one of the lessons learned from the early YouTube era was that simple, careless, joking clips were not that interesting. Although you can still have fun, people take video content more seriously these days. Your videos don't have to be super-professional or produced by a slick ad agency but they must be done well and properly organized to attract and connect with the YouTube community.

And you do want to connect with viewers to move your video higher in YouTube rankings, gain traction, and—yes!—go viral. The best place to be on YouTube is, of course, the home page. If enough viewers start watching your video, start ranking it highly, and putting it on their Favorites list, YouTube may very well highlight it on the home page or at least tag it as an editor's pick. Even if you don't make the home page, your video can still be among the most discussed, the most viewed, or the Favorites that viewers see when they click on those YouTube tabs.

We've found that the best time to launch a video on YouTube is Sunday night, about 9:00 pm EST. Your video will be up for European viewers to watch before they go off to work or school and you'll also catch the eye of U.S. viewers winding up their weekend web activities. Once they spot your video, you want them to tell their friends, link to it, comment on it, give you feedback, and (best-case scenario) make a tribute video that plays up or off the best of your content.

It's important that viewers be able to take your content from one place and bring it to another—embed it in a Facebook or MySpace page or in a blog or a web site. YouTube allows you to make your video embeddable (and, conversely, prevent your video from being embedded elsewhere if you prefer to block this kind of transfer). Make this part of your distribution plan.

Perhaps the best way to learn about YouTube is to upload a video and experience the system's features and functionality first-hand. You'll find out how YouTube categorizes videos because you have to pick a category when uploading a video. You can include a time and date stamp and—very important—add tags so your video turns up in YouTube search results of key words.

In the process, you'll learn about the community guidelines, the terms of use, and copyright tips. Users are warned, ". . . If you've recorded something from a DVD, videotaped your TV screen, or downloaded a video online, don't post it unless you have permission." See Figure 10.1 for key points to consider when using video to build your digital rep.

---

- Be aware of what's happening on the web so you can engage stakeholders proactively rather than only on the defense.
- Create content with value for target viewers. If you post a commercial, be sure it has value as content and is not just a sales pitch.
- Know the ins and outs of YouTube distribution and rankings to maximize your impact.
- Keep videos short and enable sharing if you want them to go viral.
- Have a plan in place for building on the momentum if your video does go viral.
- Tag video content carefully to maximize search results.
- Involve your stakeholders—good ideas and content can come from anywhere.
- Aim to provoke dialogue—think about what other people can do with it . . . or in response to it. (Does your video inspire response videos?)
- Be ready to respond quickly to negative videos or comments.
- Develop a strategy for building your online video library.
- Mobile is massive, so check how your video looks on mobile screens.

---

**Figure 10.1**   Using Video to Build Your Digital Rep

## Personal and Corporate Reps on View

Spend a little time on YouTube and it's obvious that, like Soulja Boy, individuals and organizations of all sizes and flavors are building their digital reps through video. Of course, the very accessibility of YouTube can also cause unintended mischief. Here's an example from Oceanside, California.

One day when his regular classroom at El Camino High School wasn't available, music teacher Mark Lowery moved band class to the choir room. With no instruments at hand, the band couldn't rehearse, so he allowed students a little free time and made them laugh by sprawling in his chair, chin down as if fast asleep. Although this was meant as a joke, one student filmed his "nap" with her cell phone camera and posted it on YouTube, where a parent saw it and alerted the local media. The next thing he knew, Lowery was called in to tell his principal the whole story.

At that point, the principal reassured the local newspaper that Lowery, a former Teacher of the Year, was playing a joke on his students, not actually sleeping in class. No official charges were filed against Lowery. Meanwhile, the student who filmed the fake nap realized that the video was taken out of context and quickly deleted it from YouTube.[2] Because of a joke captured on a cell phone and posted on YouTube, Lowery's video rep (and that of his school) could have been dinged.

The lesson: Be careful what you say and do in public (meaning any but the most personal and confidential situations where you know you won't be photographed or videotaped). Be careful what you post on YouTube, on personal or company web sites, and on blogs. You can be yourself without hiding what you think or feel about things or covering up your personality (as if you could, in the age of YouTube), but never forget that what you say or do may be shared with the world with a click or two.

Even if you're joking, the world may not share your joke. Months before he became the Republican nominee for president, John McCain was captured on video at a VFW hall ad-libbing "Bomb

Bomb Bomb, Bomb Bomb Iran" (to the tune of "Barbara Ann" by the Beach Boys). For a time it was the most watched video on YouTube, and some people began to ask: You want to be president of the United States? McCain was joking, but the video didn't help his digital rep among many segments of the voting public.

This brings us to the question of how you can protect your digital reputation and, in extreme cases, handle a crisis online. We'll discuss this more in the next chapter.

# How to Respond to Negative Comments, Gripes, and Crises

Not only do you have to build reputation equity, you have to constantly protect and defend your digital rep. What can your investor relations staff do if false rumors about your firm are circulating on Wall Street? What if you or your company is the target of innuendos, rumors, or outright lies spread through blogs, social networking sites, or YouTube? What if your toys are found to be tainted with lead paint or a patron says she found a human finger in your chili? What if you're convicted of DUI and your record shows up on the Web? What if tiny puffs of smoke from smoldering online complaints are the only clues to tip you off that a crisis volcano is about to erupt?

Dell Hell was just such a crisis volcano. Journalism professor Jeff Jarvis coined the term a few years ago when blogging about the hoops he jumped through trying to get Dell to fix his new laptop. Jarvis had paid extra for onsite service but Dell made him send the laptop back for repair anyway—and it still didn't work properly. Jarvis complained to Dell through every avenue he could find, online and off, blogging every step of the way (see http://www.buzzmachine.com/archives/cat_dell.html). Fed up, Jarvis eventually got his money back from Dell and bought an Apple laptop.

Jarvis's blog postings about Dell Hell attracted a flood of comments from other dissatisfied customers. Within a few days, mainstream media outlets had picked up the story, fanning the flames into a full-blown crisis. Could Dell have known this storm was brewing? Another blogger wrote that he learned from a spokesperson that Dell monitored blogs and forums but had a policy of "look, don't touch." Even if Dell employees noted the complaints, they never joined the online conversations, nor did they get in touch with the complainers. Once Jarvis's complaints made their way into *Business Week* and other publications, however, Dell changed course and began reaching out to bloggers and complainers.

Here's how Jarvis summarizes the lesson companies should learn from the saga of Dell Hell: "A company can no longer get away with consistently offering shoddy products or service or ignoring customers' concerns and needs. For now the customers can talk back where they can be heard. Those customers can gang up and share what they know and give their complaints volume. Of course, they can use their reviews and complaints to have a big impact on a company's reputation and business."[1]

Fast-forward to today's Dell, which hosts forums, blogs, wikis, media galleries, and Twitter discussions (see Dell Community at http://en.community.dell.com/). It has its own YouTube channel (www.youtube.com/user/DellVlog). And it has IdeaStorm (www.ideastorm.com/), where customers suggest new features or critique existing features for Dell's consideration. "IdeaStorm is revolutionary in part because it offers a transparent, fast way to close the loop with you and lets you know what we have done with your idea," the site says. "Dell executives and managers will monitor IdeaStorm to gauge which ideas are most important and most relevant to you. We've given a Dell logo to Dell employees on the site that are providing updates and feedback in an official capacity." Not surprisingly, this site has generated much discussion among customers and influential bloggers, and Dell's efforts in total have helped boost its reputation.

## Pre-Crisis Mode

Even if your firm has never faced a full-blown crisis (or hasn't experienced one in decades), you could find yourself in the middle of a huge public problem tomorrow . . . or later today. And when that happens, your digital reputation will be on the line. Dell Hell is exactly the kind of crisis that could have been avoided if Dell had been actively listening *and* responding to online conversations before the issue achieved critical mass. Let me again quote Marcel LeBrun, CEO of Radian6, which offers tools for online listening and engagement: "You can set up, through social media monitoring, an early warning system to monitor conversations that could potentially lead to a crisis and catch issues before they go viral or before they go mainstream."

Thanks to Twitter and other tools, your window of opportunity for avoiding harm to your digital rep is fairly narrow these days. If you notice online comments posted by unhappy customers, I suspect you'll have a few minutes (maybe as long as a couple of hours) to get on the case before word spreads across the Web and around the world. Don't dawdle.

What causes a crisis? Some stem from internal problems: The heart of the crisis that led to WorldCom's meltdown was management-driven accounting fraud. Others, such as product tampering situations, have external causes. My colleague Rich Blewitt classifies crises as triggered by (1) accidents (industrial, transportation, other man-made disasters), (2) natural disasters (flood, hurricane, blizzard, and so on), (3) market situations (product failure, competition, and the like), or (4) political problems (a regulatory agency shuts down your plant or proposes rules that would limit your operations, for instance).

Because a crisis can develop at any time, smart companies are always in what Rich calls the pre-crisis stage: You stay alert to your vulnerabilities, listen to online conversations with the idea of identifying issues that could erupt into a crisis, and develop workable plans for resolving such problems quickly. You can't anticipate the unknown, of course, but you can be prepared with processes and procedures for dealing with a wide range of issues.

No matter what kind of problem you find yourself addressing, it's not enough to let the world know that you're investigating or you have the situation under control. As soon as possible, the CEO or other responsible C-level executive should become the organization's spokesperson. Your dialogue should explain your solution to the crisis or, if you're still searching for a solution, outline the concrete steps you're taking to find a resolution. And as you communicate, remember that presenting your case to the online court of public opinion is not the same as presenting facts in a court of law. In World 2.0, you have to respond quickly and succinctly, formulate messages in terms of sound bites and key points, include multimedia where appropriate, and demonstrate both transparency and accountability to maintain stakeholder trust.

Early this year, after US Airways Flight 1549 struck a flock of birds leaving New York's LaGuardia Airport and the jet made an emergency landing in the Hudson River, the airline wasted no time putting up a "Flight 1549" link on its home page. The initial postings had little detail but as more information became available, the airline added links to news releases, crew bios, video interviews, a video statement from chairman and CEO Doug Parker, telephone hotlines for passengers and crew, and more. All communications (even the videos) were brief, to the point, and full of relevant sound bites. All reflected US Airways' concern for passenger safety, its complete cooperation with official investigations, and its pride in its crew members' skill and heroism.

This accident had a happy ending—everyone got off the jet safely—but no doubt the executives at US Airways recognized that the situation could have had a much grimmer outcome and were prepared to deal with such a crisis if necessary. Given the huge number of people who used the Internet to search for information about the crash, harsh online criticism would have helped sink the airline's reputation in a click. Instead, the airline's reputation is flying high because of online and offline praise.

I also want to stress that your pre-crisis planning and actual crisis response should link back to your moral purpose. An example of this from the pre-Internet age was the way Johnson & Johnson handled the product tampering crisis in 1982. J&J has a credo that lays out, very specifically, its moral purpose (see Chapter 9); serving the needs of customers is the top priority. That's why, when J&J executives found out that several people had died after swallowing poison-laced Tylenol capsules, their solution was to recall every package of Tylenol in America and publicly (and repeatedly) warn people against using any Tylenol they might have on hand.

This is a textbook case—rightly so—because J&J's moral purpose puts the needs of its customers above those of stockholders and other stakeholders, regardless of the cost (which, for this crisis, ultimately hit $100 million). The company kept everyone informed, every step of the way, displaying transparency decades before the concept became a business buzzword. Small wonder J&J's reputation has enjoyed a halo ever since—a halo that has carried over to the Web. Even now, if you do an online search for "Tylenol crisis," you'll see what I mean.

All this goes back to the point I made in Chapter 8 that the best protection against negative comments, gripes, and lies in digital World 2.0 is to build a positive reputation ahead of time. As Zappos CEO Tony Hsieh told me: "If an unhappy customer or former employee says something bad about Zappos on the web, unless the facts are inaccurate, we really don't do anything. What we've found is that our customers or even ex-employees will generally come out and defend us because we've built such a loyal customer and employee base through our culture."

But if you haven't built such a positive rep (or even if you have), what else can you do?

## Pecked to Death by Ducks

Most of the time, your reputation won't be threatened by a major crisis. Instead, your rep faces the very real threat of getting pecked to death by ducks—nibbled by negative product reviews, unflattering blog posts, and the like.

The very worst thing you can do is threaten to silence detractors, as AT&T tried to do by warning DSL customers in its Terms of Service: "AT&T may immediately terminate or suspend all or a portion of your Service, any Member ID, electronic mail address, IP address, Universal Resource Locator or domain name used by you, without notice, for conduct that AT&T believes . . . (c) tends to damage the name or reputation of AT&T, or its parents, affiliates and subsidiaries."

Outrage broke out across the Web, and within a week an AT&T spokesperson announced, "We are revising the terms of service to clarify our intent, and the language in question will be revised to reflect AT&T's respect for our customers' right to express opinions and concerns over any matter they wish. We will also make clear that we do not terminate service because a customer expresses their opinion about AT&T."[2]

Apparently many companies are still not attuned to attacks on their digital rep, let alone prepared to mount a defense. Not long ago, academic experts Dr. Christopher Martin and Dr. Nathan Bennett researched this topic and reported their results in *The Wall Street Journal*. They were surprised to find that most managers "were either unaware their company was the subject of attacks or were taking a 'wait-and-see' approach in deciding what to do about it." Yet, as they pointed out, online attacks can "help management identify concerns of dissatisfied employees and customers."

The academics recommended that managers invite and engage the critics and, ideally, stop the criticism before it starts. "A company without a publicized mechanism to address stakeholder concerns runs the highest risk for online attacks," they wrote. "In such cases, consumers often see public Internet postings as the only way to bring a problem to a company's attention, while employees see unsigned postings as the only way to raise concerns without provoking retaliation from their managers."[3]

In times of layoffs, former employees have vented their anger on the Web, writing about insensitive managers, unreasonable demands, and unfair business practices. Few talk about the praiseworthy organizations for which they used to work. Rusty Rueff, a former human resources executive at Electronic Arts, told *The New York Times* that today "whatever you say inside of a company will end up on a blog. So you have a choice as a company—you can either be proactive and take the offensive and say, 'Here's what's going on,' or you can let someone else write the story for you."[4] While a cynic would argue that whatever the company writes is going to be partial and written to protect the company's reputation, the realist would reply that whatever an outsider or a disgruntled employee writes will be even more biased. So who are you gonna believe?

Another area that provokes negative comment—and nibbles away at the organization's good reputation—is customer service. I've talked about this in earlier chapters, but an interesting approach to solving customer service issues is the Get Satisfaction site (http://getsatisfaction.com). Founder and CEO Thor Muller says that in recent years, "the effort required to communicate with hundreds of your friends has gone toward zero. Meanwhile, the trend with big companies has been to outsource and mechanize and it's getting ever harder to get through to a live person who knows as much as you do about the problem you're trying to get help with. We're creating a kind of social network designed for companies and customers to communicate with each other."

Anyone who visits the free site can ask a question about a product or service. Sometimes another consumer answers—"Your best customers know more about the product than many people who work inside the company—certainly more than most of the low-paid, call center people who are reading from a script," Muller observes. But more and more companies are assigning employees to respond. Get Satisfaction has more than 2,500 companies in its database and about half of them participate. "When customers start to converge and talk, for many companies this is gold—real engagement with current or future customers."[5]

Or take the initiative and arrange specific online destinations to solicit *your* customers' comments and address problems before they blow up. As an example, Bank of America has designated an official Twitter rep to "help, listen, and learn from our customers" (see http://twitter.com/BofA_help). Translation: He pays attention when customers tweet about difficulties and connects them with the BofA people who can investigate and provide solutions.

Another suggestion: Buy up negative domain names—Xerox owns xeroxstinks.com, ihatexerox.net, and more than a dozen others, for example—and actively use the site to solicit customer feedback.[6] If you don't make the effort to reach out to unhappy customers in this way, they'll simply post their complaints on other sites. Wouldn't you rather be the first to know instead of the last?

## Big Company/Big Problem

Put yourself in the shoes of Michael McCain, CEO of Toronto-based Maple Leaf Foods, as he learns that his company's processed meats are involved in a deadly listeria outbreak. The company is Canada's largest meat processor, and meat products account for two-thirds of its $5 billion in annual revenue. Canadian officials have just confirmed that Maple Leaf's meats are the source of a bacterial infection implicated in a number of deaths. What do you do?

What McCain *didn't* do was stay silent, evade responsibility, or offer excuses. When the problem erupted last summer, he tackled it head-on by immediately recalling Maple Leaf's meat products and apologizing in special videos on the Maple Leaf web site and on YouTube. More than 67,000 people watched his video about the meat recall and some 750 posted comments, both positive and negative (see http://www.youtube.com/watch?v=cgk3o3AJM2U).

Another step McCain took to repair the company's reputation was to create a separate web site outlining his detailed action plan for enhancing food safety systems, a plan he also explained in a special YouTube video. He continued to apologize online, in print, and on television while simultaneously reassuring the public about the quality and safety of Maple Leaf's foods. In all, the company spent $20 million on the recall and invested millions more in new safety equipment, staff, and training.[7] I can't put a price tag on McCain's online communications, but I believe they tipped the balance in saving Maple Leaf's digital rep and restoring public confidence in its products.

In fact, five months after the crisis, Maple Leaf's reputation among customers was higher than it had been before the news broke. A survey of 4,600 customers found that before the crisis the firm had a "good" opinion rating of 74 percent and a "bad" rating of 7 percent. Immediately after the news broke of the listeria outbreak, Maple Leaf's "good" rating dropped to 57 percent as the "bad" rose to 34 percent. Within five months, however, Maple Leaf's "good" rating was up to 88 percent and its "bad" back at 7 percent.[8]

Dr. Leslie Gaines-Ross, in her valuable book *Corporate Reputation*, writes that leaders must take responsibility as the first step on the road to recovering corporate reputation. She divides the process of corporate reputation recovery into four stages: Rescue (what to do immediately, starting with getting the CEO involved); Rewind (figure out what went wrong); Restore (change the culture); and Recover (what to do to begin rebuilding).[9] The Maple Leaf Foods crisis shows what can happen when the CEO drives this process from the very beginning.

Public apologies from top executives are still relatively rare, although that's changing as greater transparency becomes the norm in World 2.0—a change for the better. To quote Peter Cleveland, CEO of Cleveland Leadership Group: "A really strong leader creates a culture of accountability. Sometimes that means stepping forward and saying, 'I screwed up.'"[10]

That's how Peter Simons, president of La Maison Simons department stores in Quebec, reacted when his company's reputation was threatened. As soon as the chain's Fall 2008 back-to-school catalog appeared, some 300 customers e-mailed to complain that the models were too thin. "I stewed about it for about 36 hours, but, hey, I made a mistake," said Simons. He ordered all remaining catalogs pulped, removed the images from the store's web site, and issued an apology online. "It hurt, but I didn't care about the money, really. I was disappointed in myself and thought we could have done better."[11]

## Neutralizing Negative Comments

One way to deal with people who malign your digital reputation, of course, is to sue them. Barbara Bauer, a literary agent in New Jersey, took that route, saying in a lawsuit that critical comments in Wikipedia, on blogs, and in YouTube videos were ruining her reputation and hurting her business. An attorney representing Wikipedia told the Newark, NJ, *Star-Ledger*: "She's gone after everyone. She has sued everybody who she can identify who has said anything about her on the Internet."

There may be times when legal action makes sense, but beware—from the perspective of your digital rep, it can be wildly counterproductive, particularly if critics are careful about documenting the practices and do not allege criminal activity. Worse, lawsuits get people talking. In this case, anyone who wants to find comments about Barbara Bauer's business activities now has a wealth of sources. As one writer commented on the *Star-Ledger*'s online story, "Good word of mouth brings her business. Bad word of mouth costs her business. She can't have it both ways . . . Maybe she should take the criticism and try and correct what they are saying. Not just suing them." Wikipedia's lawyers argued that the site is not liable for comments posted by users, and a New Jersey superior court judge agreed, tossing out Bauer's lawsuit.[12]

Another approach an individual or a small business can use to neutralize (or minimize) negative material on the web is to hire a company like ReputationDefender.com, ReputationHawk.com, or MyOnlineRep.com. ReputationDefender's stated goal is to search out all the information that appears online about clients (individuals, families, companies); help remove inaccurate, inappropriate, hurtful, and slanderous information; and help control how others perceive clients online.

Michael Fertik, ReputationDefender's CEO, has an interesting observation about how people react to attempts to defend digital reputation. "If you are an individual being slammed on the web," he tells me, "other people understand that maybe some material should not be on the web because it will haunt you for the rest of your life. But there is some sense that companies are fair game for public comment."

Dan Gillmor, founder and director of the Knight Center for Digital Media Entrepreneurship at Arizona State University's Cronkite School of Journalism and Mass Communication, points out that what people say online should be viewed in context: "If every person's reputation depends on the one stupid thing he or she said—where it's not part of the pattern—then everyone will have a bad reputation and that's absurd. We all have to learn that it's not too reasonable to assume that what someone said online is the sum of that person."

Don't expect all negative content to disappear if you hire a reputation defense firm. Quoting from ReputationDefender's FAQs: "Newspaper articles and court records are difficult to impossible to remove, and we do not seek to remove them. We focus on our clients' privacy and reputations. This means we typically focus on content that is slanderous, private, defamatory, invasive, and/or outdated."

If they cannot actually remove the material (and MyOnlineRep doesn't even try, saying "removing existing information from the web ranges from difficult to impossible"), these reputation protection services can flood search engines with positive information so the negative is buried. If you wanted to do it yourself, which is time-consuming but possible, I'm told that the process would work something like the following.

## Recovering Your Own Digital Rep

Assume your name is all over Google, Yahoo!, and other search engines—and not in a good way. You're mentioned in damaging newspaper articles, like literary agent Barbara Bauer or developer Chick Edwards, and these are available on the Web. Readers have piled on with their comments and bloggers have added their views, so your name is mud and these negatives are at the top of search results.

To change how you appear on the Internet, you have to push down the relevance of these negative results and give Google and the other search engines positive new content to post. You can't erase the old and you can't make the news channels remove an article just because you don't like it and it's hurting your reputation. You have to create fresh content.

The first step is to do exhaustive searches of yourself to find not only text but also images, sound, and video results. Know what's being said about you and where your name appears, whether it's on Amazon, MySpace, Facebook, LinkedIn, Plaxo, Topix, Flickr, YouTube, a national news web site, a local media site, and so on. These are also the kinds of sites where you can get positive material posted by participating in conversations, creating profile pages, reviewing products, and commenting on news articles.

Always use your real name so search engines can find all this fresh positive content connected with your name. Update any old information a site has about you, like an Amazon account or a LinkedIn profile, but consider using privacy settings to keep some details (address, phone number, birthday) private. You don't want to hide yourself from the world, you want to publicize yourself, but on your terms.

If you haven't already registered on Facebook, MySpace, LinkedIn, Topix.com, Plaxo, and other social media sites, set up your pages now. Setting up a blog of your own is a no-brainer, but it may take some time for the search engines to pick it up. Be sure to write new posts regularly so the search engines learn to seek out your new material and include it in search results. What to post? You might write neutral articles on the day's news or your life. Or post positive comments about products or companies you deal with every day.

Post reviews on Amazon, on retail sites, on consumer sites, on YellowPages.SuperPages, on Merchants Circle. Be consistent in posting a new review every week or so, always under your own name. What are you interested in? Find those forums online and get into the conversation.

People—HR departments, college admissions officers—will still be able to find all the old negative material about you, but over time, it gets buried deeper and deeper in the search results under your new content. "If it's on the third page of Google, it basically doesn't exist," ReputationDefender's Michael Fertik explains. "Even though you can't get it off the web, getting it below the first or second page of Google means it doesn't exist."

On the other hand, as Harvard's Dean of Admissions William Fitzsimmons says, if it's public record, it's fair game. Some searchers are not going to stop at the first few results. Prospective employers, for instance, are likely to go far into the search results when doing a background check. This means you have to constantly feed the machine to try to keep your new positive content high in the search results. Today you'll review a book and write on your Facebook wall; a day or two later, you'll write a blog post and comment on someone else's blog.

Reputation recovery doesn't happen overnight. It might take months for new positive content to rise to the top of the results.

Meantime, have a system in place to remind yourself of when and where to post on a regular basis and keep monitoring your results.

Ultimately, you're in charge of making your digital reputation what you want it to be. If you do nothing to restore your personal reputation, you allow the rest of the world to control how anybody views you online. But with time, research, and effort, you can minimize the damage of an unthinking moment or some youthful (or adult) indiscretion.

If you work for a business, large or small, don't think all you have to do is send out a steady stream of positive news releases to recover your reputation. In Chapter 12 I'll talk about how World 2.0 is affecting that public relations staple, the news release.

# CHAPTER

## 12

# The New Craft of Public Relations

This book's argument has been that in World 2.0, the task of "managing" a company's reputation through the flow of information has changed dramatically thanks to technology. The PR function has always been about identifying key stakeholder audiences, guiding and facilitating conversations between the organization and its publics, adding content when needed and relevant, and helping shape public opinion for the organization's benefit. It's the *craft* of PR that is changing as the technology changes.

## Brave New PR World

For one thing, PR now has many more channels and opportunities for engaging the public on the fast-mushrooming social media side as well as in traditional media. Sorting out the possibilities is a key challenge these days: Who are the most influential or most-read bloggers and tweeters for our industry and our stakeholders? Where should we be placing content or posting comments? What are the top e-communities, and where should we participate for the best effect? Who's talking about us and what are they saying? How can we best function in the digital environment and integrate our efforts with product marketing, investor relations, and the rest of the organization?

Also, in the digital age, news cycles have been dramatically shortened and, in fact, your company's actions, statements, and reputation are actually under media scrutiny 24/7. PR is operating in what is effectively a never-ending global news cycle. There's no time off for good behavior, no reputation vacation. Nor can you simply issue periodic announcements that your company has done something you consider noteworthy.

Given how quickly news—both bad and good—can spread through the Web, you may not be able to wait for press releases or ads to have an impact anyway. You need to be in regular dialogue with stakeholders about what you're doing as a company and where you're going. You need to be constantly listening and responding to what other people say about the organization, the good and the bad.

With the rise of social media, you have less control over what's being said but more ways to get your message across. You're dealing with an ever-expanding universe of citizen journalists as well as official news media outlets, which means you don't have to rely on traditional media to be intermediaries for your messages. At the same time, you're faced with PR dialogues increasingly laced with opinions and more focused on celebrities.

In short, the rapid evolution from traditional public relations to the new craft demands mastering the online tools for managing reputation equity.

## New PR Clay: Rich Media

Marijean Lauzier, the president and CEO of the Racepoint Group, one of my companies, has given the future of PR a lot of thought. She tells me: "The old packet of information was the press release or the press kit, but that packet is changing. If the 'clay' used by advertising and interactive departments has been the visual, the 'clay' used by PR and public affairs departments has been the textual. Now PR and public affairs organizations will have to learn to work with a new 'clay'—rich media," she tells me. "Text documents and electronic presentations will certainly have a place, but communications will evolve to incorporate much more application of rich media such as video and podcasts. Technology is allowing us to create a full experience as we share news."

Social media is clearly bringing editors, reporters, and other media people online as a community, encouraging engagement and participation in information exchange. But they aren't the only people joining the PR conversation, says Marijean: "Another fundamental change is coming as collaborative technologies enable constituents to participate in the creation of company communications, react to communications, and shape the future of communications." This means that senior executives who are accustomed to controlling PR messages will have to learn to accept their lack of control in World 2.0.

Digital dialogue is, of course, an effective way to bring the public into public relations. Earlier this year, Microsoft started a new blog, Microsoft on the Issues. Now blogs are nothing new for Microsoft, which has thousands of bloggers posting from inside the corporation. But this one caught my eye because it's a public relations/public affairs blog with a very ambitious agenda for dialogue.

The company's general counsel, Brad Smith, wrote in the blog's first post: "Today we are launching 'Microsoft on the Issues' to open another, more direct line of communication that will enable us to quickly and succinctly provide our perspective on the pressing technology matters of the day. We do not want this to be a one-way conversation. We want to create a transparent dialogue with readers and stakeholders. We want to enhance our participation in discussions that propel policy-making at local, national and international levels." You can read more at http://microsoftontheissues.com/cs/blogs/mscorp/default.aspx.

Some of the posts at this blog mirror white papers and essays posted elsewhere on Microsoft's sprawling web presence. These are posts by high-level people (who also, presumably, read the comments). The point is that this blog turns what was one-way communication into a dialogue with anyone and everyone who cares to participate. The last time I looked, comments left by readers ranged from eruptions of general anti-Microsoft sentiment to thoughtful paragraphs about the issues to general support for keeping the conversation going.


## The Death of the Press Release

I claim—not without a certain amount of opposition from my colleagues—that companies don't need press releases any more. The traditional press release is to public relations what the typical 30-second commercial is to advertising: One-way communications broadcasting static content controlled by the organization. No audience input about distribution, no real dialogue.

Still, press releases are a highly efficient way to get your message out in a consistent way. Properly done—without a heavy dose of spin—they can serve as the basis of informative news stories. My point is that, in World 2.0, management simply can't hide behind a printed press release.

In reporting quarterly or annual results, a CEO now has the tools to reach out online (in a webcast, for example), explain the situation, and take stakeholder questions. Maybe the conversation would go something like this: "This was a difficult year, and you can post questions for me right now. I'll answer you for the next hour. But I'd also like to show you something exciting, take you along on a visit to a customer in France so you can see how they're using our new product."

Public companies have to report financial results to shareholders, but they can meet that legal obligation with a copy of their Form 10-K. An online annual report with top management talking seriously, responsibly, and sincerely about the issues can be much more effective than a President's Letter in a four-color, heavy stock, annual report that begins something like, "Although this past year's sales and revenue have been disappointing, our long-term prospects have never been stronger. With the recent changes in place. . . ." Not convincing. And a press release based on the letter? Not convincing.

For the longest time, PR people would send out a press release based almost entirely on the headline. They expected an editor to take it off the fax machine or out of the envelope and hand it to a reporter, who sifted through the verbiage to figure out the real story. Is the organization trying to hide something? Is it promoting something that may not be entirely beneficial? The situation reflected a serious lack of trust.

Those days are gone. When my company sends out a press release for a client (and we still do send some), we send it directly to specific reporters with a very tailored cover note that taps into each journalist's interests. In my experience, if you target individual reporters and hit them with the right information at the right time, you'll hear from them right away. Press releases done well will continue to be highly effective and stimulate conversations with media people and with your stakeholders. Poorly done press releases will be deleted in a click.

Moreover, digital press releases can contain key words that link to other relevant information. If you're writing about a machinists' strike at Boeing, you can link to other articles that either support your case or add neutral information. You can set up a Delicious.com (formerly del.icio.us) landing site where, if you are Boeing, you will have six pieces of company information supporting your case, and on and on. The digital press release becomes a much more sophisticated, multi-layered tool than yesterday's one-size-fits-all printed news release.

## Google's Press Center

Although the new craft of PR is still evolving, some companies are already retooling their activities for World 2.0. Google has started moving in that direction, as you can see if you go to its home page; click "About Google," and then click the "Press Center" link. The top box on the Press Center page features the Google Blog, written by internal experts and mostly touting the latest site enhancements. Many entries (but not all) include videos, images, and other accompaniments; all include links to more information, specific examples, and so on. Although no comments are accepted, there are other opportunities for dialogue within the Press Center, as I'll discuss in a moment.

The middle box is devoted to News from Google. Interestingly, entries marked with an asterisk are news releases (which mean they contain media contact details); all others are "announcements." This box is where Google's PR people post the positive stories they want to distribute and official responses to unexpected developments that might ding the company's digital rep.

In World 2.0, even tiny problems with a big search engine are big news and a big PR challenge. Not long ago, Google experienced a one-hour technical glitch in which the notation "This site may harm your computer" was shown beneath every search result. In what must have been a stressful hour, the tech people raced to fix the glitch while an explanation signed by Marissa Mayer, VP, Search Products & User Experience, was posted on Google News. The post was updated a few minutes later with additional details. This incident was widely reported by blogs and media outlets, but so was Google's explanation (its reputation intact).

Back on the Press Center page, the bottom box, "Google Users Say," is devoted to user testimonials. Google clearly understands the value of accentuating the positive (which I advocate in Chapter 8) by inviting users to talk about their positive experiences with the company and its goods and services. Note the placement: Google wants members of the media to see these user testimonials whenever they click to the Press Center, which I think is a smart move.

Since Google owns YouTube, it makes sense to point media reps to the Google Channel (the link is to the left on the Press Center page). Somebody's watching because when I last checked, the channel had more than 61,000 subscribers and nearly 3 million views. Best of all, comments and ratings are allowed—and I can see from the entries that people from around the world are joining the conversation.

On the right side of the Press Center page is the usual media contact information, plus a box to opt-in for an e-mail subscription to Google News. There's also a link to the Multimedia Press Room, the mother lode of media, with images, videos, documents, and webcasts—must-haves for the new craft of PR. Finally, I notice that the entire Press Center echoes the clean, spare look of Google search pages, a clear sign that Google understands the power of a well-coordinated digital strategy.

## The New News

Because the future of public relations is influenced, in part, by the future of news journalism, I talked with Dan Gillmor, at Arizona State's Cronkite School of Journalism and Mass Communication. He sees "a more useful ecosystem developing, where people had only been an audience will now be part of the journalism. With so much more information, people will have to find ways to sort through, identify the best information and quality sources, figure out what they can and can't trust."

This means PR professionals will have to become acquainted with the new journalism sites that are challenging traditional news outlets. Freed from the overhead costs of printing presses or TV cameras, these sites are very focused on local issues that range from investigating cases of possible corruption to following neighborhood zoning changes. Sites like ProPublica.org, NewHavenIndependent.org, and Crosscut.com are just a few of these new news sites.

They'll also have to get to know the bloggers who keep a close eye on particular issues of interest, on the company itself, or on the industry. For instance, the Disney Blog isn't an official company blog—it's written by uber-fan John Frost—but it has an influential voice because it attracts about 100,000 visitors each month. Frost and the fan community who read his blog have a lot to say (both positive and negative) about Disney's theme parks, products, movies, operations, management, and so on.

In an interview with social media expert Paul Gillin, Frost said that he often gets news leads from readers who comment and e-mail him (that "collaboration" thing I mentioned earlier). His posts quote his sources and include links so readers can get more background information if they choose. In short, his blog represents a new news site for fans of all things Disney.

In this interview, Frost made some good points about dealing with PR in what I see as the transition to World 2.0: "Some [corporate divisions] still won't deal with blogs, some are beginning to reach out. But our primary audiences are—and I use this term endearingly—the super geeks. They have different needs than the average consumer.

PR may only release one photo and no concept art, no details on the background story or interviews with the creator. Mass media gets all that at the press junkets, but I'm not invited, nor can I afford to attend events like that. Why would I want to repost the press release that [my readers] can get anywhere?"[1] Why indeed?

## Beyond Eyeballs

When the Web was young, ad equivalencies were a key metric in measuring the impact of online PR. Sometimes management would hear vague talk about how PR attracts eyeballs, builds awareness, and connects with customers. Those days are gone, says Racepoint's Marijean Lauzier: "Measurement will become the new currency. We're leaving an era in which the norm was loose or qualitative-only accountability for public relations departments. Public relations has to build a new literacy in analytics and in measurements. An anecdotal or qualitative discussion will no longer be sufficient in articulating the value proposition and ROI for public relations."

In World 2.0, you now have more options for measuring the nuances of your relationships with various "publics." You can quantify the reaction that your PR content and contacts generate. You can count how many bloggers mention your company's name and in what context. You can count the number of links to your content, the number of views of your YouTube videos, and the number of times your content shows up in search results. You can tally up the number of comments on your video or blog, the number of people subscribed to your content, the number of people who follow your tweets, the number of people who Digg your content on Digg.com, and so on.

This is just the beginning. You can also figure out how stakeholders find you online, map the sites or pages they were visiting just before they joined your conversation, follow their navigation across your content, and see how sticky your content really is. You can see exactly what search terms are being used to find your content. And, of course, you can track changes in search results to see how high your highlighted content moves in results rankings. This is especially important when you're trying to push positive news to the top to crowd out negative news.

Through monitoring and listening, you can determine whether you're actually engaging the stakeholders you want to reach. You can analyze the content of online dialogues to understand how stakeholders think and feel about important issues and how they respond to your company's position. We're way beyond eyeballs here, stepping into the realm of hearts and minds where reputation is really shaped.

All of these evaluation techniques can help you assess your reputation situation and focus your PR efforts on the destinations/content that are most meaningful to your stakeholders and your business. Even more precise measurement of online PR impact will soon be possible with the emergence of new tools and new technology. (In World 2.0, I expect influential PR bloggers will be the first to break the news about new tools and techniques.)

## PR and Moral Purpose

I should say a few words about PR and moral purpose. Of course your company should be a good corporate citizen, support community causes, and offer a helping hand after hurricanes or other disasters. That hasn't changed in World 2.0, nor should it. What has changed is your ability to make a real difference by enlisting stakeholders in your organization's underlying moral purpose.

Forget the old idea of photographing the CEO handing a check to the company's favorite charity or touting corporate participation in a trendy social cause when your reputation needs a boost. According to famed strategy guru Michael E. Porter and corporate social responsibility expert Mark R. Kramer, "Perceiving social responsibility as building shared value rather than as damage control or as a PR campaign will require dramatically different thinking in business."[2]

This is heavy going, but please bear with me for a moment. As I said in Chapter 9, to have shared value, your moral purpose must be meaningful to society at large and to your stakeholders—especially your employees—in particular. It also has to be fully integrated with your corporate strategy and the way you do business over the long term. In other words, your moral purpose has to be an ongoing win-win-win for society, your stakeholders, and your business.

The new tools of PR can help you manage reputation equity by better communicating your company's moral purpose and more effectively rallying internal and external support for it. But you've got to start with substance and commitment. The best PR in the world can't inspire and involve stakeholders if your organization doesn't live and breathe its moral purpose every day.

## Timberland Meets the Public

Timberland understands the "shared value" concept I just mentioned and engages stakeholders online with moral purpose in mind. Here are the opening lines of its "About Us" web page: "Our mission is to equip people to make a difference in their world. We do this by creating outstanding products and by trying to make a difference in the communities where we live and work."

Now here's how the company introduces its online press release page: "A lot happens around here on an average day. New product ideas are tossed around. Boots and shoes are designed. New fabrics are tested out. Employees participate in community service events. And that's just at our headquarters. Throw in hundreds of retail locations around the world, and there's always news being made." Anybody looking for company news will immediately recognize that moral purpose is an integral part of Timberland's business.

Timberland's news pages are fairly traditional, but it does use rich media to get the word out about its moral purpose. The company maintains an Earthkeeper blog, an Earthkeeper Twitter site, and an Earthkeeper Facebook page to publicize environmentally conscious issues and activities. It's also on YouTube, where an early "Calling All Earthkeepers" video has been viewed more than 184,000 times.

The company takes stakeholder input very seriously. In the process of developing a long-term strategy for corporate social responsibility, it solicited ideas and feedback from hundreds of stakeholders. It set ambitious goals for making products recyclable, reducing its carbon footprint, ensuring a safe and fair workplace, and encouraging community volunteer work—all issues that are meaningful to stakeholders and contribute to Timberland's positive digital rep.

## Getting Organized

I've talked a lot about the new craft of PR, but will there even be such a thing as a PR department in World 2.0? Just as Patrick Townsend and Joanne Gebhardt titled their 2000 book *Quality Is Everybody's Business*, I argue that reputation is everybody's business. What every employee says and does affects the organization's reputation. It always has, of course, but it did not have the impact it can today. One of top management's tasks is to help every member of the organization understand that how they conduct themselves influences the company's reputation.

In fact, PR has already converged with marketing, which itself is the influence of opinion through content. I define branding as the dialogue you have with your constituencies. The stronger the dialogue, the stronger your brand. Similarly, the stronger your dialogue with stakeholders, the stronger your reputation.

Now that the rise of digital content has virtually supplanted the one-way content of the past—the press release, the photo op, the pseudo event—PR is going to be the defining marketing technique of the next few years. Why? Because public relations has in its DNA the understanding of how content influences opinion.

Assuming that someone or some department must ultimately be responsible for the new craft of public relations, where in the organization should it report? My choice would be the chief marketing officer (CMO), if the CMO is a true strategic partner to the CEO (and not simply the advertising manager with a pretentious title).

You'll notice I'm not suggesting a CPRO (Chief PR Officer). I regret all the "C" titles we have in American businesses. It seems that every time a department gets a little pear-shaped, business slaps a "C" title on it. This way of thinking goes back to the Chief

Technology Officer days. They bought so much software the company needed a Chief Information Officer. Now the fastest growing C-level title in American business is that of Chief Marketing Officer.

In this case, I see the CMO's organization as the proper umbrella for PR because marketing and PR must work together on the company's digital relationships and digital content. That is, if the CMO understands marketing as dialogue and PR's importance to the firm's digital rep. Ultimately, of course, a business's digital strategy will reach way beyond traditional marketing to involve planning, research, product development, sales, customer service, and more.

As far as organizing for PR is concerned, companies need to avoid two big mistakes. One is appointing a manager deeply steeped in traditional one-way advertising as the head of a marketing or communications group. As I pointed out in Chapter 6, we're starting to see job titles change to VP of Content, VP of Community, Directors of Social Media, and so on. To fulfill and supervise these roles, you need people who are comfortable with outside criticism, who understand the company can no longer control the message, and who can engage diverse stakeholders in ongoing conversations about the business.

The second mistake is to have the web site under the information technology department. These are people who know how to build engines, not relationships, and the future of your digital rep is based on relationships. Your web site is not about technology; it's about information, connections, networks, friends, loyal customers, and more. It should be directed and managed by communications people who are steeped in the art of content and conversation creation.

Your reputation is part of an ongoing dialogue, now more public and more global than ever in history. Technology has let that genie out of the bottle and you're never going to stop the conversations. When companies stop having dialogues or lose their objectives of shaping opinion through content, people lose interest in the company and in its reputation. And having no reputation is almost as bad as having a poor one. Don't make that mistake.

Chapter 13 draws reputation lessons from the masterful digital strategy that helped propel Barack Hussein Obama's successful presidential campaign.

# Reputation Lessons from the Obama Campaign

Digital rep has such game-changing power that it can make or break a presidential candidate. Even if you're not planning to run in 2012, I think you'll appreciate the reputation lessons learned from President Barack Obama's effective campaign strategy. And if you are planning to run, you'd better start polishing your digital rep right now.

"Obama's campaign created the textbook of how to do online campaigning," says Alexis Rice, project director of CampaignsOnline .org and Fellow at the Center for the Study of American Government at Johns Hopkins University. "Every campaign, from now on—Republican, Democrat, independent, local level, state level, national level—will look to the Obama campaign as a model of how to do it right."[1]

Internet strategist Peter Daou, who ran Hillary Rodham Clinton's online campaign initiatives, agrees. After Obama clinched the Democratic nomination, Daou commented, "Theirs is an operation that everyone will be studying for campaigns to come." Obama's digital strategy actually has broader implications beyond politics. Andrew Rasiej, founder of Personal Democracy Forum, says: "Obama's success online is as much about how our society has changed, how our media ecology has changed, just in the past four years."[2]

## Early Lessons

Much of what the Obama campaign did online grew out of Howard Dean's 2003 digital campaign strategy. Neither YouTube nor Twitter existed at the time, and Facebook was just starting out, so social networking was much more limited. Still, Dean's team used the web tools at hand to rally his supporters and encourage campaign contributions. The lesson that Washington's conventional political wisdom drew from this experiment? "Howard Dean failed, and therefore the Internet didn't work."[3]

Fast-forward to the 2008 presidential race, where Dean's lessons were clearly in evidence. Coming into primary season, all of the major candidates had web sites, and the Internet was an integral part of the fall campaign for both Obama and McCain. What made Obama's digital strategy special?

First, Obama understood that the Internet *did* work, especially for mobilizing a grassroots movement. In his own words: "One of my fundamental beliefs from my days as a community organizer is that real change comes from the bottom up. And there's no more powerful tool for grassroots organizing than the Internet."[4]

Second, as Marc Andreessen has pointed out, Obama was willing to push the digital envelope. Andreessen, a Netscape founder and a Facebook board member, told *The New York Times:* "Other politicians I have met with are always impressed by the web and surprised by what it could do, but their interest sort of ended in how much money you could raise. He was the first politician I dealt with who understood that the technology was a given and that it could be used in new ways."[5]

Alex Castellanos, a Republican media consultant whose clients have included Mitt Romney and President George W. Bush, said, "You can see the main difference between the Obama and McCain campaigns by going to their Web sites. Go to McCain's. Pretty standard. Looks fine. But go to Obama's. At the very top, there's a quote: 'I'm asking you to believe. Not just in my ability to bring about real change in Washington . . . I'm asking you to believe in yours.'"[6]

Another Republican consultant, David All, observed that the McCain organization was playing to an older base, and seemed not to have grasped the impact of recent communications technology. "You have an entire generation of folks under age 25 no longer using e-mails, not even using Facebook; a majority are using text messaging. I get Obama's text messages, and every one is exactly what it should be. It is never pointless, it is always worth reading, and it has an action for you to take. You can have hundreds of recipients on a text message. You have hundreds of people trying to change the world in 160 characters or less. What's the SMS [short message service] strategy for John McCain? None."[7]

Obama's digital presence at the height of the 2008 campaign outstripped McCain's on many measures, according to the Pew Research Center's Project for Excellence in Journalism. Obama had twice as many YouTube videos posted as McCain; Obama's YouTube channel had eleven times as many subscribers as McCain's channel. Also, Obama had six times as many MySpace friends as McCain and five times as many Facebook supporters. As early as July 2007, Pew's research concluded that Obama's site was "emerging as one of the most advanced" of the candidate sites, while McCain's site was "lagging far behind."[8]

So the first lesson of the Obama campaign? The person at the top has to be enthusiastically engaged in the strategy. A CEO may not—probably should not—be involved in the specific tactics, but he or she must understand the value of a good digital reputation and push for an appropriate strategy.

The second lesson? Build a killer web site with easy-to-use e-community features.

## Welcome to MyBO

When Obama needed an e-community home base, he turned to Blue State Digital, founded by three former Howard Dean campaign workers. The company used every lesson learned from the Dean campaign—plus the latest social media bells and whistles—to develop an eye-catching, sticky, viral site nicknamed MyBO (short for My.BarackObama.com).

The site hosted all the basic one-way messages that any good campaign would want to communicate. It outlined Obama's positions on dozens of issues, from civil rights to women, with the economy, health care, and taxes in between. It featured text and video bios and speeches. And it included statements from various groups—Asian-Americans, Americans abroad, rural Americans, and 20 other groups—explaining why they supported Obama.

Even more important, MyBO was designed to engage the electorate, one voter at a time. An "Obama Everywhere" box listed the many social media sites where visitors could find Obama's profile and become his friend: Facebook, MySpace, YouTube, Flickr, Digg, Twitter, LinkedIn, Eventful, BlackPlanet, Faithbase, Eons, Glee, MiGente, MyBatanga, AsianAve, and DNC Partybuilder. It worked. Two months before the election, Obama had more than 1.7 million friends on Facebook, while McCain had just over 309,000 friends.[9] By Inauguration Day, Obama's Facebook profile showed more than 4.6 million friends (he's added more since then). At that time, John McCain had nearly 600,000 Facebook friends and Sarah Palin had nearly 500,000 Facebook friends.

Friending the candidate barely scratched the surface of MyBO's functionality. David Talbot, writing in *The Boston Globe,* said: "Newcomers to MyBO found simple, intuitive ways to get involved. You could click a button to donate. You could see maps displaying locations and details about area house parties. You could, of course, organize your own event and download the Obama message du jour. You could establish your own fund-raising efforts. And after you surrendered your e-mail address, you would get messages signed by everyone from Michelle Obama to Al Gore, with new exhortations as the primary and general election campaigns progressed."[10]

The site also encouraged dialogue. Obama campaign staffers monitored MyBO, but they didn't stop people from posting criticisms of Obama's positions. For example, MyBO users angered by Obama's compromise on the Foreign Intelligence Surveillance Act, a telecom immunity bill, formed what for a time became the single largest network group on the site. "President Obama, Please Get FISA Right" still has more than 23,000 members and 103,000 blog posts.

The Students for Obama network, another highly active group on MyBO, jumped into the dialogue with gusto. During the campaign, this nationwide network logged more than 170,000 blog messages, organized nearly 20,000 grassroots meetings, and raised more than $1.7 million in contributions. Although many blog entries supported Obama's positions and decisions, dissenters also made their voices heard. In the run-up to the inauguration, for instance, some Students for Obama blogged their criticism that Rick Warren had been chosen to deliver the invocation.[11]

## Campaign Contributions Go Social

And while it's nice to have friends, it's nicer to have generous friends.

By July 2008, about 15 months after Obama had announced his candidacy, the campaign had raised more than $200 million from more than a million online donors. At the end of the campaign, Federal Election Commission figures showed that individuals had given $657 million to Obama, just about half in contributions of $200 or less.

On MyBO, donors could charge a one-time contribution to a credit card or authorize a series of monthly contributions. Or, even better, they could make "giving money a social event," according to David Talbot. "Supporters could set personal targets, run their own fundraising efforts, and watch personal fund-raising thermometers rise."[12]

As Joe Rospars, Obama's new-media director (and founder of an Internet fundraising firm), said after the primaries: "We've tried to bring two principles to this campaign. One is lowering the barriers to entry and making it as easy as possible for folks who come to our Web site. The other is raising the expectation of what it means to be a supporter. It's not enough to have a bumper sticker. We want you to give five dollars, make some calls, host an event. If you look at the messages we send to people over time, there's a presumption that they will organize."[13]

This is the third lesson of the campaign: People need something (or a lot of things) to talk about and something to do, the proverbial call to action. MyBO gave them messages and more—a mission to raise money. "The amazing MyBO money machine," Joshua Green wrote in *The Atlantic*, "attracted large and small donors alike, those who want to give money and those who want to raise it, veteran activists and first-time contributors, and—especially—anyone who is wired to anything: computer, cell phone, PDA."[14]

## Clicking for Friends

In the post-election excitement, it was easy to forget that Obama was a relatively unknown junior senator from Illinois when he announced his presidential candidacy. He had to campaign for months against a well-connected, well-known, and (relatively) well-financed Hillary Clinton to win the Democratic nomination. He had to convince people that he was qualified to lead a country that was engaged in two wars, had a deteriorating economy, and a flawed health care system. This is where Obama's savvy use of social media came into play.

Obama was all over the Web, on the social networking sites, on YouTube, and on Twitter. "The campaign, consciously or unconsciously, became much more of a media operation than simply a presidential campaign, because they recognized that by putting their message out onto these various platforms, their supporters would spread it for them," says Andrew Rasiej, founder of the Personal Democracy Forum. "We are going from the era of the sound bite to the sound blast."[15]

Obama was the first candidate to post his profile on social networking sites for the Asian, Latino, and black communities. His popularity on BlackPlanet was so great, for example, he was able to have a different profile for each state, tailored to that state's issues. "Some people only go to MySpace," says Scott Goodstein, external online director at Obama for America. "It's where they're on all day. Some only go to LinkedIn. Our goal is to make sure that each supporter online, regardless of where they are, has a connection with Obama. Then, as much as we can, we try to drive everyone to our site."[16]

By the end of the campaign, Obama had 3.8 million supporters on Facebook; more than a million friends on MySpace; 151,000 subscribers on YouTube (uncounted millions of views, however); 491,000 friends on BlackPlanet; 165,000 followers on Twitter. While it's impossible to draw a straight line from these figures to November votes, there should be no question that—even aside from the money—all this social networking helped build Obama's digital reputation.

Let me be clear that Obama's success was *not* due to the number of friends he amassed on all these sites or the number of YouTube views his videos enjoyed. The real lesson here is that Obama engaged people on important destination sites and then invited them to MyBO for more dialogue and interaction. In other words, he went to other people's parties and brought his new friends back to his place, making MyBO the life of the party, if you'll pardon my pun.

At the same time, of course, Obama had to defend his reputation.

## Fighting the Rumor Mill

Perhaps because of Obama's color, perhaps because of his background, perhaps because of the hurly-burly of a presidential campaign, the rumor mill seemed particularly active. *Candidate Obama is a secret Muslim. He's not a natural-born American citizen. He refuses to pledge allegiance to the flag. He associates with left-wing radicals like Bill Ayres, a former terrorist and unrepentant member of the Weather Underground. Money for his campaign comes from Saudi Arabia, Iran, and other Middle Eastern countries* (as Maureen Dowd reported in *The New York Times*, yet!). All of these are false, even the Maureen Dowd citation.

Ugly rumors come with candidacy. *McCain was the father of an illegitimate black baby. He was not a native-born American citizen because he was born in the Canal Zone. He and his wife wrote a congratulatory letter to John Hinckley, the man who wounded President Reagan.* All false.

In June 2008, the Obama campaign fought back by launching a Fight the Smears web site. By Election Day, the site was offering refutations of 28 different rumors, complete with links to relevant online sources and YouTube videos. Was this an effective way to fight the rumor mill? Farhad Manjoo, a staff writer at Slate.com, argued that, because the site first repeated the lie and then rebutted it, people were likely to remember the lie as true. He cited research indicating that the more familiar a lie is to us, the more likely we are to believe it.

"There's another problem with Fight the Smears: its conception that it can spread the truth 'virally,'" Manjoo wrote. "The site asks you for your friends' e-mail addresses and even your e-mail password, with which it can access all your contacts. Your friends will then receive a bland message from you—typical line: 'These assertions are completely false and designed to play into the worst kind of stereotypes'—along with a link to Fight the Smears." The flaw in this, he argues, is that people who love Obama enough to visit his web site "are unlikely to have many friends who need setting straight."[17]

I agree that Obama supporters are unlikely to believe the rumors. I also believe that people don't question a rumor if it reinforces an existing bias. *Hussein sounds like a Muslim name . . . so Barack Hussein Obama must be Muslim even if he doesn't admit it . . . and his campaign is receiving money from Iran because they want a Muslim in the White House to turn this country into an Islamic theocracy.* It's unlikely that people whose thoughts run on this track will change their minds because of posts on an Obama-supported web site or even on an independent site like Snopes.com.

For the rest of us, however, I believe that having an authoritative, reliable, and responsible place to check questionable information is necessary. Fight the Smears was a good way to present the campaign's side of the argument directly to the electorate, without editing or interruption, and let voters make up their own minds about the rumors. The site also invited visitors to submit e-mailed rumors so the Obama camp could keep an eye on the rumor mill and respond appropriately. And the site included "spread the truth" widgets for supporters to embed on their blogs or sites—another good idea.

Bottom line: Ignoring rumors allows them to spread and fester unchecked—yet another lesson about protecting digital rep that the Obama campaign put into action.

## Don't Touch That Dial

As I discussed in the YouTube chapter, video is becoming more and more important, and the Obama campaign underscores that lesson. By the time of the Democratic convention, the campaign's video group had shot more than 2,000 hours of material and uploaded more than 1,100 videos to Obama's YouTube channel. And people were watching—they spent 14 million hours with campaign-related Obama videos on YouTube alone. By one count, all the video material posted online by the Obama campaign received a total of 50 million views.

Much of the footage was what you'd expect from any political campaign: the candidate on the stump, making speeches and TV appearances, the candidate in TV commercials and online ads. Yet a surprising number were focused on Obama's supporters. "Early on, we wanted to capture the sense that this campaign is not just about Obama," said Kate Albright-Hanna, director of online video at Obama for America. Just a couple of examples: The campaign filmed some high school students reacting to Obama's race speech and profiled a few Obama volunteers in various videos.

Albright-Hannah, an Emmy award winner who formerly worked for CNN, doesn't obsess over how many times the Obama videos are viewed. "That's not the priority. One of our goals is to get people talking about what's going on in their lives and why they're supporting Barack—and hopefully not only will they watch the videos but also comment on them and forward them to relatives and friends and co-workers."[18] So here the lesson is to give people something to talk about *and* a way to expand the conversation by taking the videos viral.

By the way, one result of the online video explosion is that TV network news editors are no longer the judge and jury of what viewers can see. As long as TV news exists, sound bites will be important, but those who want the whole enchilada can now click on YouTube for more. Obama's landmark 37-minute speech on race, delivered after an uproar over his former pastor's racial remarks, is still available on his YouTube channel, both full length and edited into three shorter videos. At this writing, the longest version has been watched more than 5.8 million times.

## Texting, Texting

When Obama launched his presidential bid, campaigning by e-mail and web site was an accepted practice but campaigning via text message was not, because users pay for texts. Once again, Obama's campaign turned conventional wisdom on its head by launching the Obama Mobile text messaging program in June, 2007. (Hillary Clinton and John Edwards also used some text messaging, but not John McCain.)

By Election Day, Obama Mobile was sending texts to more than a million people. Think of the effect on Obama's digital rep.

Here's how it came about. Scott Goodstein, the PR expert who developed Obama Mobile, recognized that nearly everyone has a cell phone and takes it everywhere—especially younger voters, an important group for Obama. Goodstein also understood the importance of keeping a dialogue going with supporters and involving them in the campaign, all within the text message limit of 160 characters, roughly two sentences.

The first step was to make it easy for supporters to subscribe to Obama's texts. The campaign e-mailed supporters and asked them to text their mailing address to sign up. In return, subscribers received free Obama bumper stickers and could download any of seven ring tones and four cell-phone wallpapers (two Obama photos and two Obama logos). All were free, although the cell phone owner had to pay standard texting rates.

Notice how the sign-up text helped the campaign update and build its mailing list. It also gave the campaign more information to text supporters by state and zip code with specific calls to action (forward this message to your friends, volunteer to make phone calls to battleground states, remind friends to vote, contribute money, attend a campaign rally in your city). But would it work?

Goodstein put Obama Mobile to the test when Oprah Winfrey appeared at an Obama rally in South Carolina during primary season. The 30,000 attendees were asked to text their information to Obama—and many did. "We got volunteers out of it. We got activists out of it," he says. At every event from then on, Obama field organizers asked attendees to text their state codes to campaign headquarters so the new-media experts could better target their messages.[19]

# Dialogue in 160 Characters

The Obama campaign was careful to make texting a two-way street. A supporter who asked a question about an issue—"Iraq?" for example—received a response within an hour: "Barack has been strongly against the war since 2002. Please visit www.barackobama.com/issues/iraq . . . 2 learn more."

Some texts combined a call to action with an invitation to continue the conversation: "Watch Barack debate tonight live on CNN! 7 PM EDT. REPLY back with your name and your thoughts during & after the debate," was sent on July 23, 2007. Texts urging action were specific about what recipients should do, when, and why. "Help Barack get out the vote in Pennsylvania! If you can get to PA between now and 4/22, REPLY to this msg: TVL and your NAME (ex. TVL Ann). Please fwd msg," was sent before the Pennsylvania primary.

The most high-profile use of Obama Mobile was the 3 AM text announcing Joe Biden as the vice-presidential pick. Faithful followers who had signed up for Obama texts had the news before the media. Although the candidate's identity was real news, so was the use of text messaging to make the announcement. In fact, the campaign got extended media mileage from announcing the decision via text—which only reinforced Obama's reputation as the most tech-savvy presidential candidate in history.

The campaign further refined its cell-phone strategy with the release of a free Obama '08 iPhone app in September 2008 through Apple's online App Store. When downloaded, the app organized users' iPhone contacts according to "key battleground states" and encouraged users to make calls in support of Obama. It also provided text and e-mail messages about Obama activities; let recipients forward this info to their contacts; downloaded national and local campaign news; helped users locate local campaign events (maps and all); and offered instant access to Obama's positions on key issues.

Two more points about maintaining a text-message dialogue. First, Obama's new-media experts were well aware that supporters were paying for texts and knew that if they abused the texting privilege, supporters would be annoyed and drop out of the conversation. Second, the campaign made it easy to drop out by simply texting STOP. The lesson? Let your stakeholders (in this case, Obama supporters) decide how long they want the dialogue to last and give them the tools to both start and stop the conversation.

## Election Day and Beyond

All of Obama's electronic outreach came together in the week before Election Day with a massive get-out-the-vote effort. The Obama campaign merged MyBO data with public records showing who was registered to vote and whether those voters had cast ballots in past elections. The MyBO data included every house party a MyBO member attended, each online connection, the date and amount of each donation, and so on, giving staffers a good picture of the probable voter base.

Four days before the election, tens of thousands of Obama supporters began logging onto MyBO to dial for votes. They downloaded small batches of voter names and phone numbers, along with a script and the location of each voter's local polling place. Dialing for votes is nothing new, but MyBO made it easier and more personal than ever before. In those four days, MyBO volunteers dialed more than three million people to get out the Obama vote. I can't say for sure whether this put Obama over the top, but I'm sure it got his supporters engaged and set the bar higher for future campaigns.

Alex Castellanos, the Republican media consultant, observed almost three months before the election: "Because of the Internet, Obama has built a movement. He's leading a cause. McCain is running on his résumé. He's leading a campaign. Now what's going to win: a cause or a campaign? We don't know."[20]

Now we know.

The Obama campaign proved that social technology can build strong bonds between a leader, his organization, and his supporters. Keeping online conversations going is even more important as the new president navigates the challenges of two wars plus a troubled economy and a host of other pressing problems.

In keeping with Obama's digital rep, the Obama team established www.change.gov right after the election as a central site for discussions, input, and announcements about the transition. At 12:01 PM on inauguration day, a new blog went live on the newly-renovated www .whitehouse.gov. The blog is quite active, and posts often include rich media, but at the moment, no comments are allowed.

Obama's team also created the Organizing for America network, which uses the tools of social media to mobilize grassroots support for the president's positions. One of the first e-mails to the 13 million members explained Obama's views on the economic stimulus package being formulated. Recipients were asked to host house parties and have guests view and discuss an online video about Obama's plan. If Organizing for America succeeds in getting supporters as involved in legislative matters as they were in the campaign, it could change the political process—forever.

What about the future of reputation? Read on.

# The Future of Digital Reputation

The future holds many challenges for managing your reputation, influence, and brand—three elements that are converging to represent the total of how you act in the real world and how you act digitally. In World 2.0, it's not sticks and stones that will hurt you—it's what stakeholders think, feel, and say about you. The online listening you do, the digital content you create, and the dialogue you have with customers, employees, and other stakeholders will all determine how they see you.

What you and your company do is always where your reputation begins—fine words cannot replace dubious deeds—but you have to talk the talk as well as walk the walk. A company that ignores its critics, hides its bad news, cuts corners, or lies is liable to find its reputation shredded as ordinary people use their computers, cell phones, and other gadgets to spread the word.

## The New Reality

Yet it's clear from my meetings and conversations that many senior executives have not grasped this new reality. For example, a recent survey of more than 700 executives worldwide found that two-thirds either were unaware of or did not want to admit that some of their employees bad-mouthed their companies online.[1] Or, if executives understand that their reputations are being shaped online, they don't know quite what to do about it. Some still believe they can control what's said about the organization; many who acknowledge they've lost control are afraid to take the next step and allow free discussion.

In the face of increased demand for transparency and authenticity, executives are struggling to find the right blend of public and private content, to engage with stakeholders over real issues while protecting proprietary information. It's an uneasy juggling act for too many corporations. According to Forrester Research (and reported by Paul Gillin) the number of business-to-business blogs started by corporations dropped by nearly half between 2006 and 2007. The reason, says Paul, is that "most corporate blogs suck."

In his own blog, Paul writes: "I ran a little test of my own in October [2008], shortly after the financial markets began to melt down. I read 20 of the most prominent corporate blogs and found that only two of them—and only one in the United States—even bothered to mention the troubles on Wall Street. The extent of this disconnect was dramatized by Wells Fargo, which chose to devote an entry on September 18—the day after the Dow suffered its single largest one-day decline in history—to a travel video. Big businesses continue to avoid discussing sensitive issues in public forums." He adds that in fairness to Wells Fargo, it has since addressed the issue, "but only tangentially."[2]

A blog is not the place to express company platitudes about "difficult times," "new strategic directions," "future opportunities," and the like. Nor is it the place to tout your great products. I would say that *nobody* believed that stuff, except that another Forrester Research study found that, in fact, 16 percent of the people surveyed said they *did* trust corporate blogs. Still, corporate blogs were the least-trusted of the 18 information sources Forrester measured—even below personal blogs. (By the way, "e-mail from people you know" was the most trusted source of information.)[3] If people don't trust you, you have a reputation problem.

## The Company as Publisher

In the future, more companies will have more employees blogging as they recognize that multiple dialogues will engage more people and strengthen their reputation equity. But if you're going to blog, discuss issues your readers care about. Write about their problems. Write about industry trends that will affect them. Write about ideas they can use to save money or make money.

As small businesses and large corporations alike get more involved with digital content, they will have to think of themselves as publishers, video producers, and libraries. The best will be electronically publishing a variety of material, both basic (usage manuals, repair guides) and blue-sky (concept cars from Detroit, energy policy ideas from oil companies). Like any good publisher, they'll analyze reader reaction, listen for what the audience wants, and respond.

The best will regularly post interesting videos and podcasts that show the company and its products in a positive light. Some of the content will be news, some will be entertainment, but the most effective will be, I suspect, both informative *and* entertaining. As you look ahead to the future of your company's digital library, remember what YouTube's Suzie Reider told me: Your content is likely to be online for a very long time.

Traditional media will continue to evolve. I think the printed newspaper will just about be gone by 2020, with the exception of a handful (possibly *The Wall Street Journal, USA Today, The New York Times*). Television's fixed-schedule nightly news will follow, because people are going to want news wherever, on whatever device, whenever they want it—when they can make time for it.

The issue that hasn't been resolved is who will pay. We've learned that it is brutally difficult to get people to pay for material on the Internet. To date, most online efforts have been supported by venture capital, company investments in their own sites, and advertising. Yet many people don't like being an online advertising target (which is why Internet ad blockers exist). Social media is soft sell, or "awareness creating."

So the challenge will be to find a balance that makes sense for companies and customers. Apart from high-profile Super Bowl commercials, people are going to continue to avoid as much advertising as they can while demanding immediate, authoritative information about products, services, and companies. We'll see a lot more experimenting with paid media that is not as intrusive as the past 80 years of broadcast marketing. As always, how—and where—you communicate helps or harms your reputation.

## Be Authentic

In the future, I believe that more and more senior executives in large corporations and entrepreneurs in smaller businesses will realize that it is in their best interest to engage online with stakeholders in genuine, authentic, human ways. To quote Herb Kelleher, founder of Southwest Airlines: "You want to create an environment in which people can be themselves."[4] Applying that attitude to a company's web site, blogs, podcasts, videos, and tweets can only help build the firm's reputation.

Being authentic means admitting mistakes. Last year, when questions were raised about whether Southwest Airlines had completed all FAA-mandated inspections of its 737 jets, management initially defended the company's actions. Despite an impressive safety record and enviable profitability, the airline faced such widespread criticism that CEO Gary Kelly quickly changed course and issued a public apology. He instituted a more stringent and comprehensive safety plan, acknowledged that some travelers had lost trust in Southwest, and told *The Wall Street Journal* that the airline was "going to have to prove to the public that we deserve their trust."[5]

Kelly opened all communication lines (digital and non-digital) to listen *and* explain. The company's blog didn't just post official notices and Congressional testimony about the 737 maintenance issue, it "put all the bad stuff on there," Herb Kelleher pointed out.[6] Let me add that Southwest is on Twitter, it's on Facebook, Flickr, YouTube, and LinkedIn.

In the future, people will continue to make mistakes, bad things will happen, and your reputation will suffer or survive depending on the equity you've built and can draw upon. A firm that's done a good job of building reputation equity using online tools will be able to strengthen, protect, *and* defend its reputation when the inevitable bad news strikes.

## Real Half, Digital Half

When the Web and social media really started to take hold, I think that many C-level executives viewed it—and still do so—as just another element of doing business, like the telephone or the fax machine, like radio ads or television commercials. From my perspective, they're just a piece of the business puzzle. I argue that the puzzle doesn't have eight pieces or a thousand, but only two: the real half and the digital half.

The real half includes the company's personnel and office, factory, showroom, store, trucks, airplanes, computers, machinery, inventory, and all the other tangible things an enterprise requires. The digital half includes the web site, the company blogs, the company intranet, and its presence on the Internet. The two halves are equally important. In fact, I think the digital side will become more important, because of its immediacy, accessibility, transparency, and connectivity as more people gain access to the Web.

That will continue to change the way companies' reputations are built—and lost. Company managements have to understand that from now on they will have to participate in the conversations that affect themselves, their companies, their industry, and their moral purposes. They don't have to have a dialogue with everyone, just with those who are most important to the organization.

Speaking of moral purpose, Gary Hamel's recent *Harvard Business Review* article, "Moon Shots for Management," puts that at the top of his wish list for reinventing management. Here's how he phrased the challenge: "Ensure that management's work serves a higher purpose. Management, both in theory and practice, must orient itself to the achievement of noble, socially significant goals." I certainly agree.[7]

## Future of Social Media

Social media is the general term covering all the things I've talked about throughout this book: Internet- and mobile-based tools for discussing and sharing information among people. Ravit Lichtenberg, an Internet strategy consultant and founder of Ustrategy.com, observes that social media was the term du jour in 2008. "Consumers, companies, and marketers were all talking about it. We have social media gurus, social media startups, social media books, and social media firms. It is now common practice among corporations to hire social media strategists, assign community managers, and launch social media campaigns, all designed to tap into the power of social media."

I agree with Lichtenberg's assessment that social media is bringing a human element to digital relations; that people will look for tangible and relevant value in their online activities; that advertisers will lose money until they understand what appeals to people who are conversing, connecting, and expressing; and that the use of social media is going to spread beyond early adopters to the mainstream.[8]

In the future, customers will be even more active participants in online company communications. Tara Hunt, author of *The Whuffie Factor: Using the Power of Social Networks to Build Your Business*, told *Fast Company*: "Web 2.0 is the participatory web—which means that the power of this time is that we are all producers. In former days of marketing, companies delivered messages and goods and customers were meant to consume them. Not so much any longer. Customers are major players in the arena of marketing—I would argue more so than the marketing professionals themselves now—so it is important to realize that and shift the marketing program to be more about how you interact and empower those customers rather than how you control and spread the message."[9]

We'll continue to see social networks develop around industries and traditional business models, with customers looking for content that, if done right, reinforces the organization's reputation. People will continue to rely on friends and network recommendations to cut through the clutter of ads and heavy-handed marketing messages and help them streamline their decision-making. What other people say about a company, product, or service will have more impact on your reputation than anything you can say.

## Leaders Look to the Future

Leaders have to be ready for this brave new world, because the mud is going to fly. No matter how trustworthy and customer-centric you try to be, some people are going to be sniping at your reputation. Employees may complain about your company policies, unions may complain about your labor practices, environmental groups may complain about your environmental efforts.

CEOs should understand that this is World 2.0 reality and be ready to respond. (It also helps to develop a thick skin.) Ideally, they should have their own Google Alerts and not rely on the public relations or the marketing departments to hear the harsh comments.

The up-and-coming CEOs who will start being appointed in the next few years are completely comfortable with digital technology. They're buying Kindles and Sony Readers today. They're hooked on BlackBerrys. They're registered on LinkedIn, planning their business trips with Dopplr, buying from Amazon, reading business news on WSJ.com and Bloomberg.com. This is a wave of leaders accustomed to having technology as their slave, and they are going to demand that technology answer a lot of problems and make things even easier in the future.

The digital future these leaders will shape will be highly visual, which means the impact of the messages will be more emotional than ever. They understand and have probably experienced the power of online visuals; they recognize that prospects and customers expect instant access to visuals, such as YouTube videos, for informed decision-making. CEOs in companies small and large should start to immediately embrace the Web's visual capabilities and present their company news, products, processes, and their customers.

Accomplishing things in a business, no matter its size, will be more campaign-like than task-like in the coming years. Creating a new product or entering a new market will involve employees and managers working together collaboratively across departmental borders, much the way professionals come together to produce a movie or record an album.

Forward-thinking leaders already recognize that collaborative thinking can be more powerful than individual thinking in achieving business objectives—and they know the pivotal role that digital technology plays in collaborative efforts. Increasingly, these leaders will welcome and actively invite customer collaboration through social media. More company/customer collaborations are out in the open on web sites such as Dell's IdeaStorm. What these participants say and do in collaborating, their online interactions as a group and their individual comments, will affect the company's long-term reputation.

## Reputation in Your Future

The reputation lesson is that you are creating a record now that is hard (or impossible) to change once it's created. Be sensitive, thoughtful, and understanding in the content you create on your web site, blog, profile, podcasts, and videos. Remember that how you act in the digital world doesn't go away. You have to consciously shape your digital reputation.

In my experience, most great leaders are great listeners. So I argue that great companies have to be great listeners, too—and act on what they hear. The Web will make it easier and easier for you to connect with any category of people, at any time, for any reason. Clearly, a huge amount of creativity exists outside of the company, and we can and should connect with that creativity.

The Web, for the first time, gives you a practical way to tap that external creativity. People who use your products may have an idea of how to make it better, package it better, explain it better, or use it in ways that your R&D experts never imagined. You can tap into that. As your reputation for responsiveness, innovation, and value grows, you can mine this enormous resource.

Not only do you have an enormous resource, but your reputation will grow as customers and potential customers recognize that you're listening to them and accepting their ideas (or at the very least responding seriously and thoroughly). By doing so, you influence your marketplace and ultimately the way stakeholders view you.

Today, your reputation precedes you in ways that were unimaginable 20 years ago. Before my first meeting with a person or company I don't know much about, I prepare myself with a Google search. I look at what the person or company has posted and what others are saying. First impressions count—and they'll be even more influential in the years to come.

"A lot of companies care about reputation only after a crisis hits," says Kasper Nielsen, a managing partner at Reputation Institute. "Then they want to know, can you fix things? They don't integrate reputation into their everyday processes. That's dangerous. You have to do a lot of things right to build up a reputation platform."[10]

Fortunately, with the digital tools available to you in World 2.0 as an individual, a small business, or a large corporation, you can do a lot of things right. All (all!) you have to do is apply them consciously and consistently. And follow the principles I've outlined in this book. The future of your digital rep is in your hands. Use it wisely.

# ACKNOWLEDGMENTS

I am indebted to my wife, Dawn, who best encapsulated this book in three words—"Sticks and Stones." Her metaphor and support fueled the process of bringing this important text to fruition. To Wally Wood, my extraordinary co-writer, who once again lent his keen ear and skillful hand to relay the sensitive but exciting reality of our evolving digital world. Many thanks to Marijean Lauzier for her insight and counsel, and to Jackie Lustig, Jan Baxter, and Farah Hussain at W2 Group for their immeasurable dedication to this endeavor. Very special thanks to my great agent, Jill Kneerim.

This book is the second book I've published with John Wiley & Sons. As with *Marketing to the Social Web*, my editor Richard Narramore gave this book his subtle but refined touch and made it a smooth read. Thank you to him and to everyone at Wiley, including Lauren Freestone and Ann Kenny, for making the production process as painless as possible. To Mary Maki and Marian Wood for supporting Wally.

Without the contributions of a host of business leaders, academics, and specialists, this book would not be as rich as it is. Mark Fuller (Monitor), Marcel LeBrun (Radian6), Jim Nail (TMS Cymfony), Paul Levy (Beth Israel Deaconess Medical Center), Helen Clark (Chevron), Tony Hsieh (Zappos), Owen Thomas (Valleywag), Dan Gillmor (Arizona State University), Paul LaVoie (Taxi), Tony Perkins (Always On), Pauline Ores (IBM), Elliot Schrage (Facebook), Idil Cakim (Golin Harris), Reid Hoffman (LinkedIn), Chris Alden (SixApart), William Fitzsimmons (Harvard University), Gail Goodman (Constant

Contact), Rick Clancy (Sony), Suzie Reider (YouTube), Michael Fertik (Reputation Defender), Aaron Hughes (Digital Influence Group), Peter Prodromou (Racepoint Group), and Rich Blewitt not only gave their time but shared their experiences and visions for reputation management in a digital age. I am grateful they joined me in my effort to tackle the tough questions of the present and to explore the future.

Finally, and as always, I want to thank my family, especially Dawn, for their support and love of a dreamer businessman who wants to help good businesses become great.

# NOTES

## Chapter 1   Your Digital Reputation in World 2.0

1. John Trumbo. "Kennewick reservist faces landscape woes." *Tri-City Herald*, October 5, 2008, p.1; Matt McGee. "Local business owner needs serious reputation management." http://www.smallbusinesssem.com/local-business-owner-needs-serious-reputation-management/1316/
2. Ansi Vallens. "The importance of reputation." *Risk Management*, April 2008, p. 36.
3. "Seventy-one percent of consumers say the reputation of corporate America is 'poor,' but consumers will buy, recommend and invest in companies that concentrate on building their corporate reputation." http://www.harrisinteractive.com/news/allnewsbydate.asp?NewsID=1318
4. Pete Engardo and Michael Arndt. "What price reputation? Many savvy companies are starting to realize that a good name can be their most important asset—and actually boost the stock price." *Business Week*, July 9, 2007, p. 70.
5. "A conversation with Dr. Leslie Gaines-Ross." http://www.corporatereputation12steps.com/QA.html#Q1

211

## Chapter 2 Psst—Want to Know Who's Talking About You?

1. The Taco Bell story is based on: Verena Dobnik, "Rats invade NYC restaurant," *The America's Intelligence Wire*, February 24, 2007; David B. Caruso, "NYC pledges action on restaurant rats," *The America's Intelligence Wire*, February 28, 2007; Carl Macgowan, "Rats! Taco Bell vermin star in clip," *Los Angeles Times*, February 24, 2007, p.A-11; David Vinjamuri, "Taco Bell rat response is strike two for Yum," http://www.thirdwayblog.com/post-types/commentary/rats-compound-taco-bells-image-crisis.html

2. Michael Arrington, "Comcast, Twitters, and the chicken (trust me, I have a point),", http://www.techcrunch.com/2008/04/06/comcast-twitter-and-the-chicken-trust-me-i-have-a-point/, April 6, 2008.

3. "The issue: What price reputation?" *BusinessWeek*, September 23, 2007, http://www.businessweek.com/managing/content/sep2007/ca20070923_089830.htm

## Chapter 4 Building Reputation: Something to Talk About

1. The Nike+ information is based on: Jay Greene, "This social network is up and running." *BusinessWeek*, November 17, 2008, p. 74; Sean Gregory, "Cool Runnings." *Time*, Octobr 15, 2007, p. 9; Nicholas Casey, "Nike, New Coach Chase Serious Runners." *The Wall Street Journal*, December 6, 2007, p. B7.

2. http://www.onlinereputationhandbook.com/live-example-of-bad-online-reputation-management/

3. Josh Bernoff, "Time to rethink your corporate blogging ideas." Forrester Research Inc., December 9, 2008, pp. 1–6.

4. Jessica Guynn, "Techie Dishes on Google's Grub." *Los Angeles Times*, January 14, 2008, www.latimes.com; "Google's In-House Food Critic." *Food Management*, August 2008, p. 14.

5. Michelle Bernhart and Alyson Slater, "How sustainable is your business? Creating a sustainability report brings new opportunities

to advance your organization's brand and reputation in keeping with stakeholder interests." *Communication World*, November–Dececember 2007, p. 18.

# Chapter 5   Building Reputation: Where to Be on the Web

1. Bob Garfield, "Widgets are made for marketing, so why aren't more advertisers using them?" *Advertising Age*, December 1, 2008, p. 1.
2. Stuart Elliott, "A meet-up, brought to you by Huggies." *The New York Times*, March 19, 2008, p. C6.
3. Lisa Belkin, "Moms and Motrin," November 17, 2008, http://parenting.blogs.nytimes.com/2008/11/17/moms-and-motrin/?pagemode=print3
4. "Audi turns mobile phones into showrooms for Q5." *Brandweek*, December 8, 2008, p. 6.
5. Bob Garfield, "Widgets," p. 1.
6. Rachael King, "How companies use Twitter to bolster their brands." *BusinessWeek*, September 6, 2008, www.businessweek.com
7. Julia Hood, "Lutz will face a different standard in new PR role." *PR Week*, December 15, 2008.

# Chapter 6   This Means New Roles, New Jobs for Every Organization

1. Smyth appeared in "PR Professional of the Future" video by Ogilvy PR Worldwide for *PR Week* magazine's Next conference, http://www.youtube.com/watch?v=kHt6Pb61Ycs
2. Excerpted from Bill Marriott, *Marriott on the Move* blog, "Uncharted Territory" entry, January 16, 2007, http://www.blogs.marriott.com/default.asp?item=435095
3. In "PR Professional of the Future" video by Ogilvy PR Worldwide for *PR Week* magazine's Next conference, http://www.youtube.com/watch?v=kHt6Pb61Ycs

## Chapter 7 Click—*Your* Personal Reputation at Stake

1. As reported in Binyamin Appelbaum, David S. Hilzenrath, and Amit R. Paley, "All just one big lie." *The Washington Post,* December 13, 2008, p. D1.
2. Robert Frank and Tom Lauricella, "Madoff created an air of mystery," December 20, 2008. http://online.wsj.com/article/SB122973208705022949.html
3. James B. Stewart, "Common sense: The lessons to be learned from the Madoff scandal." *The Wall Street Journal,* December 31, 2008, p. D1.
4. Luis M.B. Cabral and Ali Hortacsu, "The dynamics of seller reputation: Evidence from eBay," March 2006. NYU Working Paper No. EC-06-32. http://ssrn.com/abstract=1282525
5. Barbara Rozgonyi, "How to become a subject matter expert on LinkedIn," http://barbararozgonyi-wiredprworks.com/2008/05/02/how-to-become-a-subject-matter-expert-on-linkedin-10-more-ways/
6. http://www.doshdosh.com/how-to-use-the-web-to-build-a-powerful-reputation-in-any-industry/

## Chapter 8 Can a Small Business Build a Big Digital Reputation?

1. Riva Richmond, "Look who's talking: It's tempting to dismiss online review of your business; tempting, but not smart." *The Wall Street Journal,* June 25, 2007, p. R4.
2. Anya Kamenetz, "The perils and promise of the reputation economy." *Fast Company,* November 25, 2008, http://www.fastcompany.com/magazine/131/on-the-internet-everyone-knows-youre-a-dog.html

3. Edelman site: http://www.edelman.com/news/ShowOne.asp?ID=102

4. Kamenetz, "The perils and promise of the reputation economy."

5. Stefan Michel, David Bowen, and Robert Johnston, "Customer service: Making the most of customer complaints." *The Wall Street Journal*, September 22, 2008, p. R4.

6. Fred Reichheld, *The Ultimate Question: Driving Good Profits and True Growth*. Harvard Business School Press, 2006.

## Chapter 9   Big Business, Big Digital Rep

1. The Bill Heard material is based on: Cliff Banks, "Lessons from Bill Heard's collapse." WardsAuto.com, September 29, 2008, http://wardsdealer.com/latest/lessons_heards_collapse_080929/index.html; Alan Judd, "Bill Heard Dealerships Took Risky Road," *Atlanta Journal-Constitution*, September 29, 2008, http://www.ajc.com/search/content/metro/stories/2008/09/28/bill_heard_dealerships.html; "Bill Heard's $2.2 Billion Reputation Lesson." *E-Commerce's News Blog*, http://ecommercesnews.wordpress.com/2008/10/14/bill-heard%E2%80%99s-22-billion-reputation-lesson/; April Wortham and Chrissie Thompson, "Mr. Big Volume Reaches the End of the Line." *Automotive News*, September 29, 2008, p.1.

2. Pallavi Gogoi, "Wal-Mart: 'A reputation crisis.' " *BusinessWeek*, October 31, 2006, www.businessweek.com

3. Michael Barbaro, "Unbound, Wal-Mart tastemakers write a blunt and unfiltered blog." *The New York Times*, March 3, 2008, p. C1.

4. "The CEO serves: Moral purpose and business leadership. An interview with Edward M. Kopko." *Religion & Liberty*, Fall 2007, p. 3.

5. Bill George, *Authentic leadership: Rediscovering the secrets to creating lasting value*. San Francisco, Jossey-Bass, 2003, p. 22.

6. Gary Hirshberg, *Stirring it up*. New York: Hyperion, 2008, pp. 9, 24.

7. www.jnj.com/connect/about-jnj/jnj-credo/

## Chapter 10   The YouTube Juggernaut

1. http://www.nytimes.com/2008/08/16/technology/16tube
   .html?scp=1&sq=/technology/16tube.html?8dp%202008/08/
   16&st=cse
2. Cindy Long, "Smile! You're on YouTube: Millions are sharing videos online." *NEA Today*, October 2008, p. 30.

## Chapter 11   How to Respond to Negative
Comments, Gripes, and Crises

1. BuzzMachine blog by Jeff Jarvis, http://www.buzzmachine.com/
   archives/cat_dell.html
2. Ken Fisher, "AT&T threatens to disconnect subscribers who
   criticize the company," September 30, 2007, http://arstechnica
   .com/news; Ken Fisher, "AT&T relents on controversial Terms of
   Service, announces changes (updated)," October 10, 2007, http://
   arstechnica.com/news
3. Christopher L. Martin and Nathan Bennett, "Corporate
   Reputation; What to do about online attacks: Step No. 1: Stop
   ignoring them." *The Wall Street Journal*, March 10, 2008, p. R6.
4. Claire Cain Miller, "In era of blog sniping, companies shoot first."
   *The New York Times*, November 5, 2008, p. B1.
5. Kermit Pattison, "Does a new website hold the secret to great customer service?" *Fast Company*, September 12, 2008, http://www
   .fastcompany.com/articles/2008/04/interview-muller.html
6. Emily Steel, "How to handle 'IHateYourCompany.com.'" *The
   Wall Street Journal*, September 5, 2008, p. B5.
7. "How Maple Leaf Foods is handling the Listeria outbreak." CBC
   News, August 28, 2008, www.cbc.ca/money/story/2008/08/27/
   f-crisisreponse.html
8. Chris Daniels, "Maple Leaf Foods' reputation surpasses pre-crisis
   levels, study finds," PR Week, February 2, 2009, http://www
   .prweekus.com/Maple-Leaf-Foods-reputation-surpasses-pre-crisis-
   levels-study-finds/article/126702/

9. Leslie Gaines-Ross, *Corporate Reputation: 12 Steps to Safeguarding and Recovering Reputation.* John Wiley & Sons, Inc. 2007, p. xviii.
10. Eleanor Beaton, "To err is human. To admit it is strength." *The Globe and Mail*, November 7, 2008, p. B16.
11. Ian Austen, "Models too thin? A story says yes." *The New York Times*, August 31, 2008, p. B2.
12. Kelly Heyboer, "NJ literary agent fights online critics." *The Star-Ledger*, June 30, 2008, http://www.nj.com/news/ledger/topstories/index.ssf/2008/06/free_speech_on_internet_at_iss.html; "Judge throws out literary agent's lawsuit against Wikipedia." *The Star-Ledger*, July 1, 2008, http://www.nj.com/news/index.ssf/2008/07/judge_throws_out_literary_agen.html

## Chapter 12 The New Craft of Public Relations

1. "A top blogger speaks out," *Paul Gillin's Social Media Report.* October 23, 2008, http://paulgillin.com
2. Michael E. Porter and Mark R. Kramer, "Strategy & Society." *Harvard Business Review*, December 2006, p. 13.

## Chapter 13 Reputation Lessons from the Obama Campaign

1. Grant Gross, "Obama transforms web-based politics." *PC World*, December 22, 2008, http://www.pcworld.com/businesscenter/article/155917/obama_transforms_webbased_politics.html
2. Jose Antonio Vargas, "Obama's wide web." *The Washington Post*, August 20, 2008, p. C1.
3. David Talbot, "How Obama *really* did it." *Technology Review*, September/October 2008, p. 78.
4. Brian Stelter, "Obama draws on social network of support." *International Herald Tribune*, July 7, 2008, http://www.iht.com/articles/2008/07/06/business/hughes07.php
5. David Carr, "How Obama tapped into social networks' power." *The New York Times*, November 10, 2008, p. B1.

6. Jose Antonio Vargas, "Obama's wide web." *The Washington Post*, August 20, 2008, p. C1.
7. David Talbot, "How Obama *really* did it."
8. "McCain vs. Obama on the Web." Pew Research Center's Project for Excellence in Journalism, September 15, 2008, www.journalism .org/node/12772
9. "McCain vs. Obama on the Web, Social Networking." Pew Research Center's Project for Excellence in Journalism, September 15, 2008, www.journalism.org/node/12779
10. David Talbot, "The geeks behind Obama's web strategy." *The Boston Globe*, January 8, 2009, http://www.boston.com/news/ politics/2008/articles/2009/01/08/the_geeks_behind_obamas_ web_strategy/?page=2
11. Ari Melber, "Obama for America 2.0?" *The Nation*, December 23, 2008, www.thenation.comdoc/20090112.melber
12. David Talbot, "The geeks behind Obama's web strategy."
13. Joshua Green, "The amazing money machine." *The Atlantic*, June 2008, p. 52.
14. Joshua Green, "The amazing money machine."
15. David Talbot, "How Obama *really* did it."
16. Jose Antonio Vargas, "Obama's wide web."
17. Farhad Majooo, "What's wrong with Obama's FightTheSmears. com" Slate.com, June 16, 2008, http://machinist.salon.com/feature/ 2008/06/16/fight_the_smears/
18. Jose Antonio Vargas, "Obama's wide web."
19. Kate Linthicum, "Barack Obama's text message guru talks to the Ticket." *Los Angeles Times*, January 7, 2009, http://latimesblogs .latimes.com/washington/2009/01/obama-text-msgs.html
20. Jose Antonio Vargas, "Obama's wide web."

## Chapter 14  The Future of Digital Reputation

1. "Execs worried about online reputations, survey finds." *PR Week*, February 4, 2009, http://www.prweekus.com/Execs-worried-about- online-reputations-survey-finds/article/126805/?DCMP=EMC- PRUS_Daily

2. Paul Gillin, "It's time for corporate blogs 2.0." http://paulgillin.com/2008/12/its-time-for-corporate-blogs-20/

3. Josh Bernoff, "Time to rethink your corporate blogging ideas." Forrester Research, December 9, 2008.

4. Evan Smith, "Herb Kelleher. *Texas Monthly* talks: Evan Smith sits down with . . ." *Texas Monthly*, June 2008, p. 78.

5. Melanie Trottman and Andy Pasztor, "Southwest Airlines CEO apologizes for lapses." *The Wall Street Journal*, March 14, 2008, p. B1.

6. Evan Smith, "Herb Kelleher. *Texas Monthly* talks: Evan Smith sits down with . . ."

7. Gary Hamel, "25 stretch goals for management," Harvard Business Publishing blog, February 3, 2009, http://blogs.harvardbusiness.org/hamel/2009/02/25_stretch_goals_for_managemen.html

8. Ravit Lichterberg, "10 ways social media will change in 2009," http://www.readwriteweb.com/archives/10_ways_social_media_will_change_in_2009.php

9. Allyson Kapin, "8 experts predict how Web 2.0 will evolve in 2009," Fast Company, December 8, 2008, http://www.fastcompany.com/blog/allyson-kapin/radical-tech/10-experts-predict-how-web-20-will-evolve-2009

10. George Anders, "As economy slows, reputation takes on added meaning." *The Wall Street Journal*, January 9, 2008, p. A2.

# INDEX